Mrs Beeton's
HOUSEHOLD
BOOK

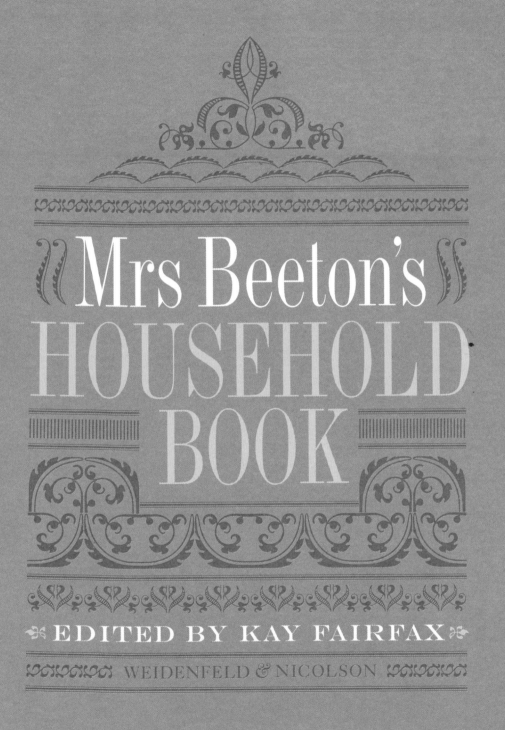

Mrs Beeton's HOUSEHOLD BOOK

EDITED BY KAY FAIRFAX

WEIDENFELD & NICOLSON

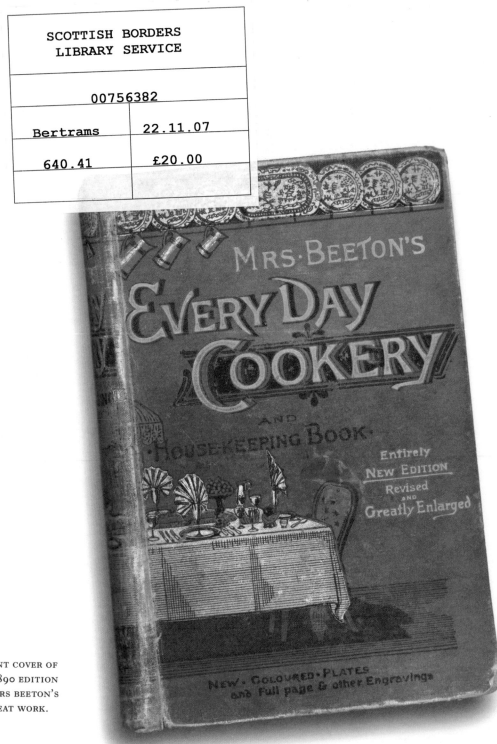

FRONT COVER OF
AN 1890 EDITION
OF MRS BEETON'S
GREAT WORK.

CONTENTS

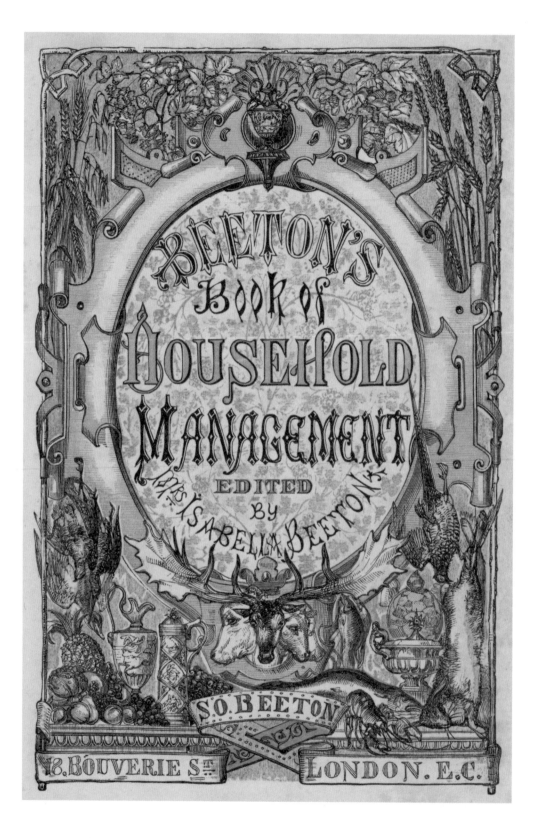

BEETON'S
Book of
HOUSEHOLD
MANAGEMENT

EDITED
BY
MRS ISABELLA BEETON

S. O. BEETON

18. BOUVERIE S.T.   LONDON. E.C.

MRS BEETON

What moved me, in the first instance, to attempt a work like this, was the discomfort and suffering which I had seen brought upon men and women by household mismanagement. [Isabella Beeton, 1836–65]

MORE THAN 140 YEARS after her death, the name Mrs Beeton is still synonymous with English cooking and many recipes today can be traced back to her original writings. The image most people have of Mrs Beeton is of a rather well proportioned middle-aged matron —in fact, she has been described as 'a slip of a girl'. Born Isabella Mary Mayson, the eldest girl of 21 children, she married Samuel Orchart Beeton, a publisher, in 1856 at the age of 20. After the death of her first child, she began writing articles for her husband's magazines, including the *Englishwoman's Domestic Magazine*, and continued to do so until her untimely death in 1865 at the age of 28 from puerperal fever, following the birth of her fourth child.

Mrs Beeton's Book of Household Management, first published in 1861, is not only a guide to the efficient running of a house in Victorian times, it is also a social history of middle-class England. According to Mrs Beeton, the mistress of the house needed to be a combination of a modern day Dr Spock, Delia Smith, Florence Nightingale, an army general and an accountant. She must also be 'perfectly conversant with all the other arts of making and keeping a comfortable home'.

Perhaps surprisingly, many of Mrs Beeton's words and advice are as relevant today as they were then. Her observations on such important issues as the huge gap between the rich and the poor, the lack of education and decent housing for the lower classes, and the importance people placed on material wealth to impress others and to create a place for themselves in society are as yet, unanswered. Today's society has many parallels, with its excess of designer labels, new cars and the latest 'must haves'. The greatest difference is that many wives and mothers are now expected to work outside the home as well as keep house. Once again, servants and nannies have become a necessity rather than a luxury and Mrs Beeton has a great many words of wisdom on how to treat domestic staff.

Even in Victorian days the wealthy took their benevolent responsibilities seriously, just as the rich and famous of today lend their names to raise money for the less well off. The Victorians were a mobile society coming from the country to the cities to improve their lot, just as today's migrants are moving across the world for a better life. They were wary of public hospitals and infection, a not unknown consideration today. They believed in herbal alternative medicine and many women preferred home births. Fresh produce was brought into the cities, mirroring the way many people today are again turning to farmers' markets for fresh food.

Mrs Beeton's advice on a women's role in family life may sound pompous and old fashioned, but her words still make a lot of sense.

'She who makes her husband and her children happy, who reclaims the one from vice and trains up the other to virtue, is a much greater character than ladies described in novels.

It is of incalculable benefit to them that their homes should possess all the attractions of healthful amusements, comfort, and happiness; for if they do not find pleasure there, they will seek it elsewhere. Let her conduct be such that her inferiors may respect her, and such as an honourable and right-minded man may look for in his wife and mother of his children.'

And her advice on clothes might be dated, but many of today's female role models could do a lot worse than heed her words.

'In purchasing articles of wearing apparel, it is well for the buyer to consider three things. I. That it is not too expensive for her purse. II. That its colour harmonize with her complexion, and its size and pattern with her figure. III. That its tint allow of its being worn with the other garments she possesses. That a good wife sets up a sail according to the keel of her husband's estate; and if of high parentage, she doth not so remember what she was by birth, that she forgets what she is by match.'

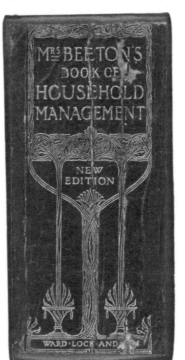

There is a constancy across the years and it is interesting to note how many of the kitchen utensils illustrated in the 1861 edition of Mrs Beeton's book are still in use. Pots and pans are virtually unchanged as is the humble cheese grater and colander. We learn that the footman was issued with a pair

SPINE OF THE 1907 EDITION OF MRS BEETON'S BOOK OF HOUSEHOLD MANAGEMENT.

of overalls, a waistcoat and a fustian jacket, with a white or jean one for times when he might answer the door. The word 'jean' refers to a twilled cotton cloth also known as serge de nim because it was made in Nîmes in southern France. Denim is clearly more universal and of longer use than the 20th century might have us think.

In Georgian times, as today, rooms were multi-purpose and furniture was often moved around the house to accommodate different functions, but with the Victorians came a much stricter sense of order. Each room became a specific space with a very definite *raison d'être,* and making the home the centre of entertainment, and family life became the most important mission in a housewife's life.

Rooms became segregated, with those used for entertaining visitors more lavishly furnished and decorated, reflecting the status and prosperity of the owners, than the more utilitarian family rooms. The drawing room was the main entertaining room for visitors, while the parlour was the sitting room for the family. The morning room was the domain of the mistress of the house and it was here that she organized the daily tasks of the household. Woe betide the mistress who did not perform her duties properly.

For this collection of Mrs Beeton's wisdom and guidance on running the home and managing servants, I have selected some of my favourite sections of her book. There is plenty of advice that is still interesting and useful for households today—as well as much that gives a fascinating insight into the lives and attitudes of the Victorians. I haven't been able to resist adding some of the passages that are amusing to us today, such as this on treating hysteria:

HYSTERIA

This may manifest itself by intense sobbing or immoderate laughter, or these may alternate with one another. There is frequently wild tossing about of the arms, the hair is dishevelled, the face is generally pale and complaint is made of a suffocating feeling in the throat.

TREATMENT. – *The patient must be spoken to kindly, yet firmly, and be told to stop any eccentricities. Loosen the dress and remove anything tight from the neck. Give a teaspoon of spirit of sal volatile in water. If no heed is taken to what is said, dash cold water upon the face.*

The advice is good – loosen the dress etc – but one can only imagine what Mrs Beeton would say about some of the 'eccentricities' of today.

To help clarify some of Mrs Beeton's advice I have added some background information on the housing, social conditions and attitudes of the time. These paragraphs are marked with a decorative bar.

Mrs Beeton's great work is far more than a recipe book or manual of household tips. It is a portrait of a nation, of a particular sector of Victorian society. As such, it is an invaluable document that more than stands the test of time.

A FAMILY
EVENING IN
A VICTORIAN
HOME.

It is not advisal
to take favourit
another lady's d

e, at any time,
dogs into
wing-room.

THE DRAWING ROOM

WHEN A VISITOR is announced the occupations of drawing, music, or reading should be suspended. If a lady, however, be engaged with light needlework, and none other is appropriate in the drawing-room, it may not be, under some circumstances, inconsistent with good breeding to quietly continue it during conversation, particularly if the visit be protracted, or the visitors be gentlemen.

The drawing room was the most important room in the house. It was the main room for receiving visitors, so established the social status and wealth of the family to the outside world. Drawing room etiquette was appropriately strict.

The furniture, paintings and artefacts in the drawing room helped establish one's place in society but just as important was the conduct of the mistress of the house. Her manners, style of dress and knowledge of correct etiquette was paramount to the successful running of the household and to being accepted in the class of society to which the family aspired or already belonged. Mrs Beeton has many words of advice on this subject, some of which are just as relevant today as they were back then.

ETIQUETTE FOR THE
MISTRESS OF THE HOUSE

The choice of acquaintances was very important to the happiness of a mistress and her family. A gossiping acquaintance, who indulged in the scandal and ridicule of her neighbours, should be avoided as a pestilence. Friendships should not be hastily formed, nor the heart given, at once, to every new-comer. Hospitality is a most excellent virtue; but care must be taken that the love of company, for its own sake, does not become a prevailing passion; for then the habit is no longer hospitality, but dissipation. With the respect to the continuance of friendships, however, it may be found necessary, in some cases, for a mistress to relinquish, on assuming the responsibility of a household, many of those commenced in the earlier part of her life. This will be the more requisite, if the number still retained be equal to her means and opportunities.

In conversation, trifling occurrences, such as small disappointments, petty annoyances, and other every-day incidents, should never be mentioned to your friends. If the mistress be a wife, never let an account of her husband's failings pass her lips. She should

[*16*]

MRS BEETON
ADVISED WIVES
NEVER TO
COMPLAIN ABOUT
ANY FAILINGS
OF THEIR
HUSBANDS.

always be good tempered and strive to be cheerful and should never fail to show a deep interest in all that appertains to the well-being of those who claim the protection of her roof. Her visitors are also pleased by it and their happiness increased.

[*17*]

Drawing room décor was a miasma of ornamentation and colour. A bare room was not acceptable and householders liked to cover every surface with objects and bric-a-brac reflecting their particular aspirations and interests, while making sure everything was correct and nothing would jeopardize their place in 'polite society'. Often this room was adorned with heavy drapes and equally heavy mahogany furniture, bought to last and 'selected because it was correct, moral, worthy, not because it was attractive'. The drawing room was generally so full of furniture and bits and pieces, that moving around often proved to be a hazard.

The choice of heavy drapes and dark colours was not just a fashion whim but one borne out of practicality, as towns and cities at this time were noisy and choked with soot from thousands of coal fires. Thick curtains helped keep out noise and rich dark paintwork didn't show the dirt so much. Even the piano was covered with felt or serge to make it a useful place to add yet more ornaments. Indeed, there is a myth that the sight of the piano's legs was held to be scandalous and for the sake of modesty they were covered with ' tiny pantalettes'. The overcrowding and large amounts of furniture not only illustrated the apparent wealth of the household but also demonstrated that there was enough seating for their many friends and callers.

An amusing episode concerning this overcrowding is related by Mrs Jane Ellen Panton, a well-known author of the time. She tells of an 'unfortunate acquaintance' who tried to join his dinner partner to escort her in to dinner. In attempting to negotiate his way around the furniture he crossed the room, 'knocking over the chair next him, and arriving at his destination with a fringed antimacassar neatly fastened to one of his coat-buttons. He then backed into a small table, on which

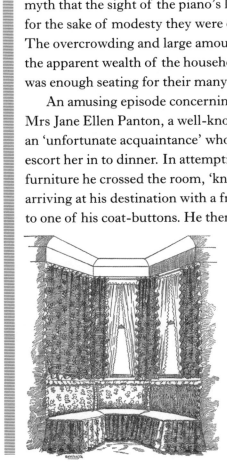

stood some books and photographs, and only saved this, to send another spinning; this time smashing the whole concern and depriving me of one of my pet flower-holders…'. But worse was to come: in one heroic effort to get away from the scene of the disaster he backed once more into a 'what-not' full of china. As Mrs Beeton said, 'a place for everything and everything in its place'.

DRESS FOR RECEIVING VISITORS

It is also of great importance for the mistress to pay strict attention to the subject of dress and fashion. The dress of the mistress should always be adapted to her circumstances, and be varied with different occasions. She must be changed from her neat and simple attire worn for breakfast and domestic occupations of the morning, to be ready to receive visitors. It is still to be remembered, however, that, in changing the dress, jewellery and ornaments are not to be worn until the full dress for dinner is assumed and as a general rule it is better to be under-dressed than over-dressed. In purchasing articles of wearing apparel, whether it be a silk dress, a bonnet, shawl, or riband, it is well for the buyer to consider three things. I. That it is not too expensive for her purse. II. That its colour harmonize with her complection, and its size and pattern with her figure. III. That its tint allow of its being worn with other garments she possesses.

To brunettes, or those having dark complections, silks of a grave hue are adapted. For blondes, or those having fair complections, lighter colours are preferable, as the richer, deeper hues are too overpowering for the latter. The colours which go best together are green with violet; gold-colour with dark crimson or lilac; pale blue with scarlet; pink with black or white; and grey with scarlet or pink.

THE HEAVY VICTORIAN STYLE CONTINUED TO INFLUENCE ENGLISH DRAWING ROOMS IN THE EARLY 20TH CENTURY.

MRS BEETON
STRESSES THAT
SERVANTS MUST
TAKE GREAT CARE
TO ANNOUNCE
VISITORS
CORRECTLY, AS
MISPRONOUNCING
NAMES IS APT TO
GIVE OFFENCE.

A cold colour generally requires a warm tint to give life to it. Gray and pale blue for instance, do not combine well, both being cold colours.

> After luncheon the mistress was supposed to be dressed and ready to receive 'morning calls'. Despite the term, morning calls were actually made in the afternoon.

MORNING CALLS AND VISITS

During these visits, the manners should be easy and cheerful, and the subjects of conversation such as may be readily terminated. These visits are usually short, a stay of from fifteen to twenty minutes being quite sufficient.

Formerly, the custom was for the lady of the house to accompany all visitors quitting the house to the door, and there take leave of them; but modern society which has thrown off a great deal of this kind of ceremony, now merely requires that the lady of the house should rise from her seat, shake hands, or courtesy, in accordance with the intimacy she has with her guests, and ring the bell to summon the servant to attend them and open the door.

If the drawing room was being used for an afternoon reception an 'At Home' card was sent to the invited guests. Only very simple refreshments were offered at these occasions, such as thinly sliced bread and butter, sandwiches, biscuits and cakes, and perhaps ice cream. No alcoholic drinks or wine, but there would be lemonade and punch as well as tea, coffee and chocolate. If the tea was later in the afternoon often the drapes would be drawn and the gaslamps lit and some form of entertainment included, such as musicians, to entertain the guests.

DRAWING ROOM ETIQUETTE FOR GENTLEMEN

IT IS SAID that Victorian etiquette dictated that it was rude for a gentleman to offer his seat to a lady, as the cushion might still be warm.

OTHER ADVICE for gentleman on etiquette when being entertained included the following: not to sit on the sofa beside the hostess, or in near proximity, unless invited to do so; avoid introducing weighty topics into the conversation such as religion or politics; make use of a handkerchief only if absolutely necessary, but without glancing at it afterwards and be as unobtrusive in the action as possible.

A MAN SHOULD always remain standing until all the ladies present are seated and he must never take any object from the hands of a lady eg. a book or a cup if he is seated and she is standing.

HE MUST never scratch his head, use a toothpick, earspoon or a comb in the presence of ladies, nor must he ever be seen to glance at his watch during the visit. He also should never laugh at his own wit, but allow others to do so and he is to remember that utmost diligence upon propriety be observed.

DRAWING ROOM ETIQUETTE
FOR VISITORS

A lady paying a visit may remove her boa or neckerchief; but neither her shawl or bonnet. When other visitors are announced, it is well to retire as soon as possible, taking care to let it appear that their arrival is not the cause.

When they are quietly seated, and the bustle of their entrance is over, rise from your chair, taking a kind leave of the hostess, and bowing politely to the guests.

Should you call at an inconvenient time, not having ascertained the luncheon hour, or from any other inadvertence, retire as soon as possible, without, however, showing that you feel yourself an intruder.

In all these visits, if your acquaintance or friend is not at home, a card should be left. If in a carriage, the servant will answer your inquiry and receive your card; if paying your visit on foot, give your card to the servant in the hall, but leave to go in and rest should on no account be asked. The words "Not at home" may be understood in different senses; but the only courteous way is to receive them as being perfectly true. You may imagine that the lady of the house is really at home, and that she would make an exception in your favour, or you may think that your acquaintance is not desired; but in either case, not the slightest word is to escape you, which would suggest, on your part, such an impression.

In making a first call, either upon a newly-married couple, or persons newly arrived in the neighbourhood, a lady should leave her husband's card together with her own, at the same time, stating that the profession or business in which he is engaged has prevented him from having the pleasure of paying the visit with her.

A visitor always had to wait to be admitted into the room and never continued the visit if the mistress of the house was dressed to go out. Visitors were also advised that they should never appear to stare, or touch anything in the room, always speak in a quiet melodious voice and never turn their back on another guest.

No dogs in the drawing room

It is not advisable, at any time, to take favourite dogs into another lady's drawing-room, for many persons have an absolute dislike to such animals; and besides this, there is always a chance of a breakage of some article occurring, through their leaping and bounding here and there, sometimes very much to the fear and annoyance of the hostess. Her children also, unless they are particularly well-trained and orderly, and the visitor is on exceedingly friendly terms with the hostess, should not accompany a lady in making morning calls.

A MISTRESS'S RESPONSIBILITIES

She ought always to remember that she is the first and the last, the Alpha and the Omega in the government of her establishment; and that it is by her conduct that its whole internal policy is regulated. Therefore let each mistress always remember her responsible position, never approving a mean action, nor speaking an unrefined word. Let her conduct be such that her inferiors may respect her and let her prove herself, then, the happy companion of man.

RECIPES TO SERVE AT TEA IN THE DRAWING ROOM

Scotch Shortbread.
Macaroons.
Thick Gingerbread.
—
Hunting Nuts.
The long-shaped nut
is found convenient for
the hunting-coat
pocket.

Meringues.
Saucer Cake for Tea.
Small Sponge-cakes.
Tea Cakes.
—
Sandwiches
—
Lemonade.
Ice Cream.

[*25*]

It has often been
was the butler w
his prospective
and not the othe

said that it

ho interviewed

mployer

way round.

THE BUTLER

T HE DOMESTIC DUTIES of the butler are to bring in the
eatables at breakfast, and wait upon the family at that meal,
assisted by the footman, and see to the cleanliness of everything at table. On taking away, he removes the tray with the china
and plate, for which he is responsible. At luncheon, he arranges the
meal, and waits unassisted, the footman being now engaged in other
duties. Before dinner, he has satisfied himself that the lamps,
candles, or gas-burners are in perfect order, if not lighted, which
will usually be the case.

The more servants a Victorian establishment employed, the more
prestige it gave them in society. Even small households would have
at least a cook and a housemaid, but the ultimate snob value was the
butler. It has often been said that it was the butler who interviewed his
prospective employer and not the other way round, and many a butler
would turn down a job if the household was not up to his standards.
He would rather be employed in a grander, more socially established
household than in a less prestigious position, even if it meant lower
wages. Many a new mistress would find herself intimidated or at odds
with the butler, who was already well established in the household.

The butler would usually be older and more mature than the rest
of the male staff, having worked his way up from a junior footman
to a first footman before reaching his present position. Having spent
several years working in more lowly positions, he would already have
been familiar with household routine and had an insight into what was
expected of him and the rest of the staff. He was always dressed as a
gentleman, in either a frock coat or morning coat, or sometimes just a
plain, well-cut black coat, worn with striped trousers and immaculate
shiny, black shoes. The family addressed him by his surname only,
such as Fletcher, while the other servants always called him Mr
Fletcher. He was very much 'above stairs' and usually only associated
with the housekeeper and cook, and maybe with the first footman, who
was training to become a butler himself.

[*29*]

At dinner, [the butler] places the silver and plated articles on the table, sees that everything is in its place, and rectifies what is wrong. He carries in the first dish, and announces in the drawing-room that dinner is on the table, and respectfully stands by the door until the company are seated, when he takes his place behind his master's chair on the left, to remove the covers, handing them to the other attendants to carry out. After the first course of plates is supplied, his place is at the sideboard, to serve the wines, but only when called on.

The first course ended, he rings the cook's bell, and hands the dishes from the table to the other servants to carry away, receiving from them the second course, which he places on the table, removing the covers as before, and again taking his place at the sideboard.

At dessert, the slips being removed, the butler receives the dessert from the other servants, and arranges it on the table, with plates and glasses, and then takes his place behind his master's chair to hand the wines and ices, while the footman stands behind his mistress for the same purpose, the other attendants leaving the room. Where the old-fashioned practice of having the dessert on the polished table, without any cloth, is still adhered to, the butler should rub off any marks made by the hot dishes before arranging the dessert. Having served every one with their share of the dessert, put the fires in order (when these are used), and seen the lights are all right, at a signal from his master, he and the footman leave the room.

He now proceeds to the drawing-room, arranges the fireplace, and sees to the lights; he then returns to his pantry, prepared to answer the bell, and attend to the company, while the footman is clearing away and cleaning the plate and glasses. At tea he again attends. At bedtime he appears with the candles; he locks up the plate, secures doors and windows, and sees that all the fires are safe.

A BUTLER HAD
HIGH STATUS IN
THE HOUSEHOLD
AND A MERE
PAGE SCARCELY
DESERVED HIS
ATTENTION.

THE
SERVANTS' MAGAZINE.

No. 13. New Series.]   1 January, 1868.   [Price One Penny.

ORDER, IN THE BUTLER'S PANTRY.

If there was no House Steward, the butler was considered the highest official employee and was in charge of running the house and was responsible for all the male servants. He would hire and fire and could make life tolerable or miserable for lesser servants. His salary was forty to sixty pounds per annum, but he would often augment this with additional 'contributions' from various suppliers of goods for the household. If a butler managed to save enough money during his working years, he might, on retirement, pool his resources with the housekeeper or cook and open a boarding house or run a small pub.

In a grand establishment where there was a servant's hall, the strictest etiquette was as important there as it was in the main house. The butler, the housekeeper, the cook and sometimes the first footman were waited on by lower-ranking downstairs servants or ate separately in the housekeeper's apartment. It was normally only the butler and the housekeeper who had the comfort and privacy of their own rooms.

As the butler had sole responsibility for the wine and plate of the household he always carried a set of keys for his pantry and never let them out of his possession.

A POSITION OF TRUST

In addition to these duties, the butler, where only one footman is kept, will be required to perform some of the duties of the valet, to pay bills, and superintend the other servants. But the real duties of the butler are in the wine-cellar; there he should be competent to

advise his master as to the price and quality of the wine to be laid in; "fine," bottle, cork, and seal it, and place it in the binns. Brewing, racking, and bottling malt liquors, belong to his office, as well as their distribution. These and other drinkables are brought from the cellar every day by his own hands, except where an under butler is kept; and a careful entry of every bottle used, entered in the cellar-book; so that the book should always show the contents of the cellar.

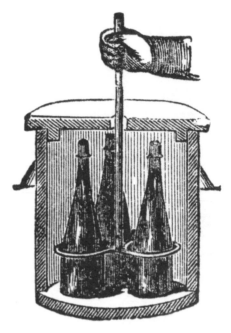

ESSENTIAL ITEMS FOR A BUTLER: A WINE COOLER (ABOVE); CHAMPAGNE OPENER (RIGHT) AND A CLARET BASKET (OPPOSITE).

The office of butler is thus of very great trust in a household. Here, as elsewhere, honesty is the best policy; the butler should make it his business to understand the proper treatment of the different wines under his charge, which he can easily do from the wine-merchant; and faithfully attend to it; his own reputation will soon compensate for the absence of bribes from unprincipled wine-merchants, if he serves a generous and hospitable master. Nothing spreads more rapidly in society than the reputation of a good wine-cellar, and all that is required is wines well chosen and well cared for; and this a little knowledge, carefully applied, will soon supply.

The butler, we have said, has charge of the contents of the cellars, and it is his duty to keep them in proper condition, to fine down wine in wood, bottle

HAVING thoroughly washed and dried the bottles, supposing they have been before used for the same kind of wine, provide corks, which will be improved by being slightly boiled, or at least steeped in hot water,– a wooden hammer or mallet, a bottling-boot, and a squeezer for the corks. Bore a hole in the lower part of the cask with a gimlet, receiving the liquid stream which follows in the bottle and filterer, which is placed in a tub or basin. This operation is best performed by two persons, one to draw the wine, the other to cork the bottles. The drawer is to see that the bottles are up to the mark, but not too full, the bottle being placed in a clean tub to prevent waste. The corking-boot is buckled by a strap to the knee, the bottle placed in it, and the cork, after being squeezed in the press, driven in by a flat wooden mallet.

As the wine draws near the bottom of the cask, a thick piece of muslin is placed in the strainer, to prevent the viscous grounds from passing into the bottle. Having carefully counted the bottles, they are stored away in their respective binns, a layer of sand or sawdust being placed under the first tier, and another over it; a second tier is laid over this, protected by a lath, the head of the second being laid to the bottom of the first; over this another bed of sawdust is laid, not too thick, another lath; and so on till the binn is filled.

Wine so laid in will be ready for use according to its quality and age. Port wine, old in the wood, will be ready to drink in five or six months; but if it is a fruity wine, it will improve every year. Sherry, if of good quality, will be fit to drink as soon as the "sickness" (as its first condition after bottling is called) ceases, and will also improve; but the cellar must be kept at a perfectly steady temperature, neither too hot nor too cold, but about 55° or 60°, and absolutely free from draughts of cold air.

it off, and store it away in places suited to the sorts. Where wine comes into the cellar ready bottled, it is usual to return the same number of empty bottles; the butler has not, in this case, the same inducements to keep the bottles of the different sorts separated; but where the wine is bottled in the house, he will find his account, not only in keeping them separate, but in rinsing them well, and even washing them with clean water as soon as they are empty.

The dress, attitude and prestige of a butler have hardly changed since Victorian days. Even today, it is considered a great cachet for the rich and famous to have a butler, in full dress, open the door to guests, and there are still many men about town who prefer to have a butler than a housekeeper or cleaner. Butlers can be hired for special occasions and there are several very successful schools for butlers to learn their trade before going on to lucrative jobs around the world in households where such a show of prestige is still considered important.

ATTENDING TO HIS MASTER'S WINES WAS A BUTLER'S MOST IMPORTANT TASK.

A BUTLER AND HIS CELLAR—FINING WINE

THERE ARE VARIOUS modes of fining wine; eggs, isinglass, gelatine, and gum Arabic are all used for the purpose. Whichever of these articles is used, the process is always the same. Supposing eggs (the cheapest) to be used,– Draw a gallon or so of the wine, and mix one quart of it with the whites of four eggs, by stirring it with a whisk; afterwards, when thoroughly mixed, pour it back into the cask through the bunghole, and stir up the whole cask in a rotatory direction, with a clean split stick inserted through the bunghole.

Having stirred it sufficiently, pour in the remainder of the wine drawn off, until the cask is full; then stir again, skimming off the bubbles that rise to the surface. When thoroughly mixed by stirring, close the bunghole, and leave it to stand for three or four days. This quantity of clarified wine will fine thirteen dozen of port or sherry. The other clearing ingredients are applied in the same manner, the material being cut into small pieces, and dissolved in the quart of wine, and the cask stirred in the same manner.

Cleanliness, pu[r]
and method, ar[e]
in the character[
housekeeper.

tuality, order,
essentials
of a good

THE HOUSEKEEPER

L IKE "CAESAR'S WIFE," she should be "above suspicion", and her honesty and sobriety unquestionable; for there are many temptations to which she is exposed. In a physical point of view, a housekeeper should be healthy and strong, and be particularly clean in her person, and her hands, although they may show a degree of roughness, from the nature of some of her employments, yet should have a nice inviting appearance. In her dealings with the various tradesmen, and her behaviour to the domestics under her, the demeanour and conduct of the housekeeper should be such as, in neither case, to diminish, by an undue familiarity, her authority or influence.

The housekeeper managed the day-to-day tasks of the household, allocated duties to the other servants, disciplined them if necessary and in many cases literally ran the house. This was especially true if her mistress was young and newly married and had never shouldered the responsibility of supervising staff, let alone knew how to keep a large establishment in order. The new mistress may have grown up in such an environment, where she had enjoyed all the privileges of her class, but might never have been greatly involved in the actual mechanics of hiring servants, ordering food and generally being in charge of a large group of people. In such a situation, an experienced housekeeper could be a young mistress's salvation, even though she may at times have felt in awe of her employee.

HER MISTRESS'S REPRESENTATIVE

As second in command in the house, except in large establishments, where there was a house-steward, the housekeeper must consider herself as the immediate representative of her mistress, and bring to the management of the household all those qualities of honesty, industry, and vigilance in the same degree as if she were the head of her own family. Constantly on the watch to detect any wrong-doing on the part of any of the domestics, she will overlook all that goes on in the house, and will see that every department is thoroughly attended to, and that the servants are comfortable, at the same time that their various duties are properly performed.

Cleanliness, punctuality, order, and method, are essentials in the character of a good housekeeper. Without the first, no household can be said to be well-managed. The second is equally all-important; for those who are under the housekeeper will take their "cue" from her; and in the same proportion as punctuality governs her movements, so will it theirs. Order, again, is indispensable; for by it we wish to be understood that "there should be a place for everything, and everything in its place." Method, too, is most necessary; for when the work is properly contrived, and each part arranged in regular succession, it will be done more quickly and more effectually.

A necessary qualification for a housekeeper is, that she should thoroughly understand accounts. She will have to write in her books an accurate registry of all sums paid for any and every purpose, all the current expenses of the house, tradesmen's bills, wages, and other extraneous matter. A housekeeper's accounts should be periodically balanced and examined by the head of the house. Nothing tends more to the satisfaction of both employer and employed, than this arrangement. "Short reckonings make long

THE HOUSE-
KEEPER NEEDED:
'THOSE QUALITIES
OF HONESTY,
INDUSTRY, AND
VIGILANCE IN
THE SAME DEGREE
AS IF SHE WERE
THE HEAD OF HER
OWN FAMILY.'

friends," stands good in this case as in others. It will be found an excellent plan to take an account of every article which comes into the house connected with housekeeping, and is not paid for at the time. The book containing these entries can then be compared with the bills sent in by the various tradesmen, so that any discrepancy can be inquired into and set right. An intelligent housekeeper will, by this means, too, be better able to judge of the average consumption of each article by the household; and if that quantity be, at any time, exceeding, the cause may be discovered and rectified, if it proceed from waste or carelessness.

Periodically, at some convenient time,– for instance, quarterly or half-yearly, – it is a good plan for the housekeeper to make an inventory of everything she has under her care, and compare this with the lists of a former period; she will then be able to furnish a statement, if necessary, of the articles which, on account of time, breakage, loss, or other causes, it has been necessary to replace or replenish.

> The housekeeper was usually a mature woman, with previous experience of her job. Often a widow, she considered herself of a higher class than the other servants, except maybe the butler. She held a position of authority and trust, which allowed for privileges well above the other servants. She had her own room and small sitting room, which no one entered except by invitation. If she had a pleasant personality and happy countenance, it would make all the difference between having cheerful, willing servants or ones who were surly and discontented in their jobs.

THE HOUSEKEEPER WAS ADVISED TO LIST EVERYTHING UNDER HER CARE, INCLUDING HOUSEHOLD GOODS AND THE BEST CHINA.

Although in the department of the cook, the housekeeper does not generally much interfere, yet it is necessary that she should possess a good knowledge of the culinary art, as, in many instances, it may be requisite for her to take superintendence of the kitchen, As a rule, it may be stated, that the housekeeper, in those establishments where there is no house-steward or man-cook, undertakes the preparation of the confectionery, attends to the preserving and pickling of fruits and vegetables, and, in a general way, to the more difficult branches of the art of cookery.

Much of these arrangements will depend, however, on the qualifications of the cook; for instance, if she be an able artiste, there will be little necessity for the housekeeper to interfere, except in the

A SELECTION OF
DELICATELY
SHAPED PETITS
FOURS SHOWED
OFF THE SKILL
OF COOK AND
HOUSEKEEPER.

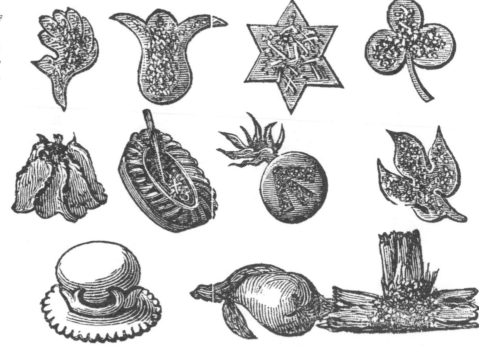

[46]

already noticed articles of confectionery, &c. On the contrary, if the cook be not so clever and adept in her art, then it will be requisite for the housekeeper to give more of her attention to the business of the kitchen, than in the former case. It will be one of the duties of the housekeeper to attend to the marketing, in the absence of either a house-steward or man-cook.

The housekeeper was often regarded rather like a headmistress, and was held in awe by the other servants. It was up to her to see that the household ran smoothly, that the servants did their jobs properly, and the ordering of supplies was kept up to date. In other words she was the manager and watchdog of everything that went on in the house. Her word was law.

THE HOUSEKEEPER'S ROOM

The housekeeper's room is generally made use of by the lady's maid, butler, and valet, who take there their breakfast, tea and supper. The lady's maid will also use this apartment as a sitting-room, when not engaged with her lady, or with some other duties, which would call her elsewhere. In different establishments, according to their size and the rank of the family, different rules, of course, prevail. For instance, in the mansions of those of very high rank, and where there is a house-steward, there are two distinct tables kept, one in the steward's room for the principal members of the household, the other in the servant's hall, for the other domestics. At the steward's dinner-table, the steward and housekeeper preside; and here, also, are present the lady's-maid, butler, valet and head-gardener. Should any visitors be staying with the family, their servants, generally the valet and lady's maid, will be admitted to the steward's table.

The housekeeper's responsibilities were even more onerous if she worked in a widower's establishment, where she might also have the children to nurture, sometimes acting as a surrogate mother, if they were young, perhaps with the assistance of a nanny. In this position she needed to act with discretion and decorum at all times in order to avoid gossip or scandal, although quite often one would hear the comment, made with much derision, 'He married the housekeeper', usually death to further social progress. Marrying the master was not unlike being commissioned from the ranks—sometimes it worked, but other times it could be regretted.

THE HOUSEKEEPER'S DUTIES

The daily duties of a housekeeper are regulated, in a great measure, by the extent of the establishment she superintends. She should, however, rise early, and see that all the domestics are duly performing their work, and that everything is progressing satisfactorily for the preparation of the breakfast for the household and the family.

SUPERVISING
THE WORK OF
OTHER SERVANTS,
SUCH AS MAIDS
AND ODD-JOB MEN,
ON THE MISTRESS'S
BEHALF WAS ONE
OF THE HOUSE-
KEEPER'S DUTIES.

After breakfast, which, in large establishments, she will take in the housekeeper's-room with the lady's maid, butler, and valet, and where they will be waited on by the still-room maid, she will, on various days set apart for each purpose, carefully examine the household linen, with a view to its being repaired, or to further quantity being put in hand to

A HOUSEKEEPER
WHO WAS SKILLED
IN THE ART OF
CONFECTIONERY
MIGHT MAKE
AN ELABORATE
CREATION SUCH AS
THIS SWISS CHALET
OF NOUGAT.

be made; she will also see that the furniture throughout the house is well rubbed and polished; and will, besides, attend to all the necessary details of marketing and ordering goods from the tradesmen.

After dinner, the housekeeper, having seen that all the members of the establishment have regularly returned to their various duties, and that all the departments are in proper working order, will have many important matters claiming her attention. She will, possibly, have to give the finishing touch to some article of confectionery, or be occupied with some of the more elaborate processes of the still-room. There may also be the dessert to arrange, ice-creams to make; and all these employments call for no ordinary degree of care, taste, and attention.

In the evening, the housekeeper will often busy herself with the necessary preparations for the next day's duties. Numberless small, but still important arrangements will have to be made, so that

Jelly of 2 Colours.

Macedoine of Fruits with Jelly

Lemon Cream

Victoria Sandwiches.

Meringues.

Grape Jelly.

Chocolate Cream.

Iced Oranges.

Trifle

Tipsy Cake

Stewed Pears.

Rout Cakes.

Crystalized Fruits.

Apples à la Parisienne

Nougat Almond Cake.

Blanc-Mange à la Vanille

everything may move smoothly. At times, perhaps, attention will have to be paid to the breaking of lump-sugar, the stoning of raisins, the washing, cleansing, and drying of currants, &c. The evening, too, is the best time for setting right her account of the expenditure, and duly writing a statement of moneys received and paid, and also for making memoranda of any articles she may require for her store-room or other departments.

SEASONAL TASKS

It will be useful for the mistress and housekeeper to know the best seasons for various occupations connected with Household Management; and we, accordingly, subjoin a few hints which we think will prove valuable.

As, in the winter months, servants have much more to do, in consequence of the necessity there is to attend to the number of fires throughout the household, not much more than the ordinary every-day work can be attempted. In the summer, and when the absence of fires gives the domestic more leisure, then any extra work that is required can be more easily performed.

The spring is the usual period set apart for house-cleaning, and removing all the dust and dirt which will necessarily, with the best of housewives, accumulate during the winter months, from the smoke of the coal, oil, and gas, &c. This season is also well adapted for washing and bleaching linen, &c., as, the weather not being then too hot for the exertions necessary in washing counterpanes, blankets, and heavy things in general, the work is better and more easily done than in the intense heats of July, which month some recommend for these purposes. Winter curtains should be taken down, and replaced by the summer white ones; and furs and woollen

ONE OF THE HOUSEKEEPER'S DUTIES WAS TO OVERSEE THE MAKING OF DESSERTS FOR SPECIAL OCCASIONS IN THE HOUSEHOLD.

clothes also carefully laid by. The former should be well shaken and brushed, and then pinned upon paper or linen, with camphor to preserve them from the moths. Furs, &c., will be preserved in the same way.

Included, under the general description of house-cleaning, must be understood, turning out all the nooks and corners of drawers, cupboards, lumber-rooms, lofts, &c., with a view of getting rid of all unnecessary articles, which only create dirt and attract vermin; sweeping of chimneys, taking up carpets, painting and whitewashing the kitchen and offices, papering rooms, when needed, and, generally speaking, the house putting on, with the approaching summer, a bright appearance, and a new face, in unison with nature. Oranges should now be preserved, and orange wine made.

The summer will be found, as we have mentioned above, in consequence of the diminution of labour for the domestics, the best period for examining and repairing household linen, and for "putting to rights" all those articles which have received a large share of wear and tear during the dark winter days. In direct reference to this matter, we may here remark, that sheets should be turned "sides to middle" before they are allowed to get very thin. Otherwise, patching, which is uneconomical from the time it consumes, and is unsightly in point of appearance, will have to be resorted to. In June and July, gooseberries, currants, raspberries, strawberries, and other summer fruits, should be preserved, and

MRS BEETON
DESCRIBES HER
RECIPE FOR
CHRISTMAS
PUDDING AS "AN
UNRIVALLED
PLUM-PUDDING".
IT WAS INDEED
EXTREMELY RICH.

Compote of Fruits.

Christmas Plum Pudding.

[52]

jams and jellies made. In July, too, the making of walnut ketchup should be attended to, as, the green walnuts will be approaching perfection for this purpose. Mixed pickles may also be made now, and it will be found a good plan to have ready a jar of pickle-juice into which to put occasionally some young French beans, cauliflowers, &c.

In early autumn, plums of various kinds are to be bottled and preserved, and jams and jellies made. A little later, tomato sauce, a most useful article to have by you, may be prepared; a supply of apples laid in, if you have a place to keep them, as also a few keeping pears and filberts. Endeavour to keep a large vegetable marrow–it will be found delicious in the winter.

In October and November, it will be necessary to prepare for the cold weather, and get ready the winter clothing for the various members of the family. The white summer curtains will now be carefully put away, the fire-places, grates, and chimneys looked to, and the house put in a thorough state of repair, so that no "loose tile" may, at a future day, interfere with your comfort, and extract something considerable from your pocket.

AUTUMN TASKS INCLUDED CLEANING FIRE-SIDE ITEMS SUCH AS COAL SCUTTLES.

In December, the principal household duty lies in preparing for the creature comforts of those near and dear to us, so as to meet Old Christmas with a happy face, a contented mind, and a full larder; and in stoning the plums, washing the currants, cutting the citron, beating the eggs, and Mixing the Pudding, a housewife is not unworthily greeting the general season of all good things.

It ought to be th
of every parent
children feel tha
the happiest pla

e policy
o make her
home is
e in the world.

THE PARLOUR

O F THE MANNER of Passing Evenings at Home, there is none pleasanter than in such recreative enjoyments as those which relax the mind from its severer duties, whilst they stimulate it with gentle delight. Where there are young people forming part of the evening circle, interesting and agreeable pastime should especially be promoted. It is of incalculable benefit to them that their homes should possess all the attractions of healthful amusement, comfort, and happiness; for if they do not find pleasure there, they will seek it elsewhere.

Family evenings would often have been spent in the parlour. In aristocratic and very wealthy establishments the grand drawing room was generally only used for entertaining important guests and on formal occasions. In houses such as these, there was another less formal sitting room, known as the parlour, which was used for day-to-day family life. This was the room the ladies would retire to after dinner, leaving the gentlemen to enjoy their port and cigars before joining the rest of the company a little later for the evening's entertainment.

In many smaller houses there was only one main formal room and this was the parlour. It was this room by which the status of the family was judged by society and where the show of wealth was most important. Often these rooms were only used for entertaining guests or by the family on Sundays. The Victorians believed that the more furniture and accoutrements one could cram into a room the more it impressed their guests. The parlour was furnished in much the same way as described for the drawing room, but as the rooms were of smaller dimensions they tended to appear even more cluttered and over-furnished. There was usually a round table in the centre of the room, covered with a cloth on which to serve tea. There were numerous, mostly uncomfortable, chairs for guests, knick-

MUSICAL
EVENINGS IN THE
PARLOUR WERE
A FAVOURITE
FORM OF ENTER-
TAINMENT AND A
YOUNG LADY WAS
EXPECTED TO BE
AN ACCOMPLISHED
PIANIST.

knacks everywhere, domes filled with stuffed birds and the inevitable aspidistra plant, whose leaves had to be polished every day by some poor housemaid. If the family was musical, there would be a piano, covered with more paraphernalia, and a music stand. There was also a grandfather clock, a mirror above the fireplace, and family portraits, or fashionable prints, hung on the walls.

These rooms often appeared gloomy, as the woodwork and the walls were usually of a dark colour, the furniture was mostly mahogany and there were heavy drapes on the windows. These thick curtains were important, not only because they acted as a deterrent for the large amount of dirt and dust outside, but also because Victorians did not consider sunlight beneficial for the furniture or for people.

MUSICAL EVENINGS

It ought, therefore, to enter into domestic policy of every parent to make her children feel that home is the happiest place in the world. To imbue them with the delicious home-feeling is one of the choicest gifts a parent can bestow. Musical evenings make additional attractions for home, and increase its pleasures. Where music is cultivated by the mistress of a house or by the daughters, husbands and brothers are generally found "at home" in the evenings.

Playing the piano was an expected part of female accomplishments and the harp was also a popular musical instrument among the feminine members of the household. Gentlemen would often sing duets, accompanied by one of the ladies playing the piano, but they would very seldom play it themselves, as it was considered only suitable for a lady or a professional musician. As Lord Chesterfield was heard to remark some years earlier, 'that if a man loved music he should pay fiddlers to play for him but never make himself appear frivolous and contemptible by playing himself.'

[59]

EVENING PURSUITS

Light or fancy needlework often forms a portion of the evening's recreation for the ladies of the household, and this may be varied by an occasional game at chess or backgammon. It has often been remarked, too, that nothing is more delightful to the feminine members of a family, than the reading aloud of some good standard work or amusing publication. A knowledge of polite literature may be

thus obtained by the whole family, especially if the reader is able and willing to explain the more difficult passages of the book, and expatiate on the wisdom and beauties it may contain. This plan, in great measure, realizes the advice of Lord Bacon, who says, "Read not to contradict and refute, nor to believe and take for granted, nor to find talk and discourse, but to weigh and consider."

If there were enough members or friends of the family gathered, they would often play charades or indulge in a game of cribbage, chess or backgammon for an hour or so, until tea was brought in around ten o'clock. After which the young would retire, followed by the ladies of the house. The gentlemen, if there was a library, billiard or smoking room, would don smoking jackets, caps and slippers and retire to their inner sanctum to read, play billiards and to smoke. Smoking in female company was not considered proper and it was ungentlemanly to smell of smoke. As prosperity increased, billiard rooms were added to smaller establishments and the more adventurous ladies learnt the game. But not everyone approved of these pursuits and it was said that: 'Proficiency at billiards is the sign of a misspent youth'.

THE PARLOUR-MAID

A parlour-maid is kept in many households in place of a single foot-man, and in these cases her duties are practically the same as his, with attendance on her mistress in place of that given by him to his master. In some households a single man-servant and parlour-maid are both kept, but where there is more than one man-servant she is not needed, as they do all the work of answering the door, waiting at table &c. In many families of good income a parlour-maid is pre-ferred to a man-servant, as giving less trouble, doing more work, and where no lady's-maid is kept, being available for some small services for her mistress and waiting upon her when required. In households of three servants (the other two, cook and housemaid, with perhaps, a kitchen-maid beside) she is most often found, and in such a household it will be best to detail her work.

The duties of the parlour-maid are, as we have before said, very much the same as those of the single man-servant. She opens the door to visitors, shows them to the drawing-room, brings up afternoon tea, and clears it away, lays the table for luncheon and dinner, and waits during the latter meal, with or without the assistance of the house-maid; she keeps the linen in repair, waits upon her mistress, assisting her to dress when required, also upon any lady visitor. She has often to help in bed-making, and is gen-erally required to dust the drawing-

COLLECTING THE CUTLERY FROM THE TABLE AND KEEPING IT CLEAN AND IN GOOD CONDITION WAS ONE OF THE PARLOUR-MAID'S RESPONSIBILITIES.

ARRANGING
FLOWERS FOR THE
HOUSE WAS
ANOTHER OF THE
PARLOUR-MAID'S
TASKS.

room, often to arrange the flowers for that and the dining-room, to put up fresh curtains, look after the drawing-room fire, and answer the sitting-room bell. She washes up the breakfast, tea and coffee things, and the glass and plate from dinner, and the plate is under her charge to be kept clean and in order. She does, in fact, all the lighter and less menial work of a housemaid, combining with many little tasks that a mistress who kept only two servants would in all probability do for herself.

DRESS

A parlour-maid is always required to dress nicely; no heavy or dirty work falls to her share, therefore she should always be neat and clean. As a housemaid, her morning attire should be a print gown and simple white cap, but she will not need the rough apron worn by the former, and can wear a white one, so that she is always ready to answer bells. In the afternoon her dress should be a simply-made black one, relieved by white collar, cuffs, and cap, and a pretty lace-trimmed bib apron.

[*63*]

WAITING AT TABLE

The parlour-maid should move about the room as noiselessly as possible, anticipating people's wants by handing them things without being asked for them, and altogether be as quiet as possible. It will be needless here to repeat what we have already said respecting waiting at table in the duties of the butler and footman: the rules that are good to be observed by them, are equally good for the parlour-maid. If there be a man-servant in attendance, he takes the butler's place and she the footman's, as already detailed; if the housemaid assists, then the parlour-maid takes the first place.

EVENING WORK

Dinner over, the parlour-maid removes the plates and dishes on the tray, places the dirty knives and forks in the basket prepared for them, folds up the napkins in the rings, which indicate by which member of the family they have been used, brushes off the crumbs on the hand-tray kept for the purpose, folds up the table cloth in the folds already made, and places it in the linen-press to be smoothed out. After every meal the table should be rubbed, all marks from hot plates removed, and the table-cover thrown over, and the room restored to its usual order. If the family retire to the drawing-room, or any other room, it is a good practice to throw up the sash to admit fresh air and ventilate the room.

She will now have to wash up the plate and glass used, restoring everything to its place; next prepare the tea and take it up, bringing the tea-things down when finished with, and lastly, give any attendance required in the bedroom.

MANY A GENTLE-
MAN ENJOYED
A QUIET EVENING
READING BY THE
PARLOUR FIRE.

Before sweeping
it is a good prac
it all over with t

:he carpet,
ice to sprinkle
-leaves...

THE MORNING ROOM

IT IS THE CUSTOM of 'Society' to abuse its servants, — a *façon de parler*, such as leads their lords and masters to talk of the weather, and, when rurally inclined, of the crops, — leads matronly ladies, and ladies just entering on their probation in that honoured and honourable state, to talk of servants, and, as we are told, wax eloquent over the greatest plague in life while taking a quiet cup of tea.

The morning room was the place where the mistress saw her servants and issued instructions for the daily running of the home. This was her inner sanctum. She would discuss the ordering of the food and the menus for the day with the cook and instruct the housekeeper on any particular requirements, such as the arrival of house guests or entertainment that might need special attention. Here she would also interview new servants and supervise the household accounts. Once these tasks were completed the mistress would spend considerable time in writing letters and answering, or sending invitations.

As this room was daily under the close scrutiny of the mistress, her

A GOVERNESS BEING INTER-VIEWED BY THE MISTRESS OF THE HOUSE.

comfort and pride in it was foremost in her mind, so the housemaid needed to make sure it was up to standard before the mistress entered. The maid would open the drapes, sweep, dust and, in winter, clean the grate and lay the fire. Only then was it ready for the mistress to enter and begin her daily routine.

ON CLEANING

Before sweeping the carpet, it is a good practice to sprinkle it all over with tea-leaves, which not only lay all dust, but give a slightly fragrant smell to the room; rubbing tables and chairs, dusting the mantel-shelf and picture frames with a light brush, dusting the furniture and sweeping the rug. It is not enough, however, in cleaning furniture, just to pass lightly over the surface; the rims and legs of tables, and the backs and legs of chairs and sofas, should be rubbed vigorously daily; if there is a bookcase, every corner of every pane and ledge requires to be carefully wiped, so that not a speck of dust can be found in the room

Morning visitors, usually close friends or relatives, were received in the morning room. They would take light refreshment and pass the time in a little harmless gossip while carrying on with genteel activities such as sewing, embroidery, or pressing flowers. Particularly popular at this time was Berlin woolwork.

The room itself was often decorated in a lighter, softer and more feminine style than the other rooms in the house and would include a Davenport, or small writing desk, and comfortable chairs. Several of the chairs would be without arms to accommodate the dress styles of the day, as the crinoline and the bustle were not made for sitting comfortably for any length of time. Often there would be a credenza, showing off the mistress's favourite pieces of porcelain, a small piano with a mahogany canterbury and perhaps one or two pieces of papier-mâché.

ADVICE FOR THE MISTRESS ON HIRING SERVANTS

CLOSE FRIENDS AND RELATIVES WERE RECEIVED IN THE MORNING ROOM.

There are few families of respectability, from the shopkeeper in the next street to the nobleman whose mansion dignifies the next square, which do not contain among their dependents attached and useful servants; and where these are absent altogether, there are

[*71*]

THE MISTRESS
WOULD OFTEN DO
HER ACCOUNTS
AND TAKE CARE
OF OTHER
BUSINESS AT
A SMALL WRITING
DESK IN THE
MORNING ROOM.

good reasons for it. The sensible master and the kind mistress know, that if a servant depend on them for very many of the comforts of life; and that, using a proper amount of care in choosing servants, and treating them like reasonable beings, and making slight excuses for the shortcomings of human nature, they will, save in some exceptional case, be tolerably well served, and, in most instances, surround themselves with attached domestics.

It is another conviction of "Society" that the race of good servants has died out… that there is neither honesty, conscientiousness, nor the industrious habits which distinguished the servants of our grandmothers; that domestics no longer know their place

Engaging domestics is one of those duties in which the judgement of the mistress must be keenly exercised. One of the commonest modes of procuring servants is to answer advertisements inserted in the newspapers by those who want places; or to insert an advertisement, setting forth the kind of servant that is required. In these advertisements it is well to state whether the house is in town or country, and indicate pretty closely the amount of wages that the mistress proposes to give. There are some respectable registry-offices, where good servants may sometimes be hired. Another plan, and one to be recommended under certain conditions, is for the mistress to make inquiry amongst her circle of friends and acquaintances, and her tradespeople. Shopkeepers generally know those in their neighbourhood who are wanting situations, and will communicate with them, when a personal interview with some of them will enable the mistress to form some ideas of the characters of the applicants, and suit herself accordingly.

EXPECTED DUTIES

We would here point out an error—and a grave one it is—into which some mistresses fall. They do not, when engaging a servant, expressly tell her all the duties which she will be expected to perform. This is an act of omission severely to be reprehended. Every portion of work which the maid will have to do should be plainly stated by the mistress, and understood by the servant. If this plan is not carefully adhered to, an unseemly contention is almost certain to ensue, and this may not be easily settled; so that a change of servants, which is so much to be deprecated, is continually occurring.

A SERVANT'S CHARACTER

In obtaining a servant's character, it is not prudent to be guided by a written one from some unknown quarter; but it is better to have an interview, if at all possible, with the former mistress. By this means you will be assisted in your decision as to the suitableness of the servant for your place by the appearance of the lady and the state of her house. Negligence and want of cleanliness in her and her household generally will naturally lead you to the conclusion that her servant has suffered from the influence of the bad example.

BY THE END OF
VICTORIA'S REIGN
THE STYLE WAS
BECOMING LESS
CLUTTERED.

The proper course to pursue in order to obtain a personal interview with the lady is this; — The servant in search of the situation should be desired to see or write to her former mistress, and ask her to be kind enough to appoint a time, convenient to herself, when you may call on her; this proper observation of courtesy being necessary to prevent any unseasonable intrusion on the part of a stranger. Your first questions should be relative to the honesty and general morality of her former servant; and if no objection is stated in that respect, her other qualifications are then to be ascertained. Inquiries should be very minute, so that you may avoid disappointment and trouble, by knowing the weak points of your domestic. Your questions also should be brief, as well as to the point.

TREATMENT OF SERVANTS

The treatment of servants is of the highest moment, as well to the mistress as to the domestics themselves. On the head of the house the latter will naturally fix their attention; and if they perceive that the mistress's conduct is regulated by high and correct principles, they will not fail to respect her. If, also, a benevolent desire is shown to promote their comfort, at the same time that a steady performance of their duty is exacted, then their respect will not be unmingled with affection, and well-principled servants will be still more solicitous to continue to deserve her favour.

In giving a character, it is scarcely necessary to say that the mistress should be guided by a sense of strict justice. It is not fair for one lady to recommend to another, a servant she would not keep herself. The benefit, too, to the servant herself is of small advantage; for the failings which she possess will increase if suffered to be indulged with impunity.

[75]

HOUSEKEEPING ACCOUNTS

A HOUSEKEEPING account-book should invariably be kept, and kept punctually and precisely. The plan for keeping household accounts, which we should recommend, would be to enter, that is, write down in a daily diary every amount paid on a particular day, be it ever so small; then, at the end of a week or month, let these various payments be ranged under their specific heads of Butcher, Baker &c; and thus will be seen the proportions paid to each tradesman, and any week's or month's expenses may be contrasted with another. The housekeeping accounts should be balanced not less than once a month—once a week is better; and it should be seen that the money in hand tallies with the account.

Once a month it is advisable that the mistress overlook her store of glass and china, marking any breakages on the inventory of these articles.

WHEN, in a large establishment, a housekeeper is kept, it will be advisable for the mistress to examine her accounts regularly. Then, any increase of expenditure which may be apparent can easily be explained, and the housekeeper will have the satisfaction of knowing whether her efforts to manage her department well and economically have been successful.

ON MARKETING

In marketing, that the best articles are the cheapest, may be laid down as a rule; and it is desirable, unless an experienced and confidential housekeeper be kept, that the mistress should herself purchase all provisions and stores needed for the house. If the mistress be a young wife, and not accustomed to order "things for the house", a little practice and experience will soon teach her who are the best tradespeople to deal with, and what are the best provisions to buy.

Frugality and economy are home virtues without which no household can prosper. Dr. Johnson says: "Frugality may be termed the daughter of Prudence, the sister of Temperance, and the parent of Liberty. He that is extravagant will quickly become poor, and poverty will enforce dependence and invite corruption." The necessity of practising economy should be evident to every one, whether in the possession of an income no more than sufficient for a family's requirements, or of a large fortune, which puts financial adversity out of the question. We must always remember that it is a great merit in housekeeping to manage a little well. "He is a good waggoner," says Bishop Hall, "that can turn in a little room. To live well in abundance is the praise of the estate, not of the person. I will study more how to give a good account of my little, than how to make it more."

In this there is true wisdom, and it may be added, that those who can manage a little well, are most likely to succeed in their management of larger matters. Economy and frugality must never, however, be allowed to degenerate into parsimony and meanness.

In great houses
carefully match
like a pair of ca
must be exactly

hey are
ed: the footmen,
riage horses,
the same size.

THE FOOTMAN

WHEN A LADY of fashion chooses her footman without any consideration than his height, shape, and tournure of his calf, it is not surprising that she should find a domestic who has no attachment for the family, who considers the figure he cuts behind her carriage, and the late hours he is compelled to keep, a full compensation for the wages he exacts, for the food he wastes, and for the perquisites he can lay his hands on.

There are many amusing stories about the footman. Despite Mrs Beeton's views, many employers seemed to consider his appearance more important than his ability to perform his job properly. His physique was often the main reason he was hired and the taller and more handsome he was the more salary he received. Even better were brothers who looked alike and the ultimate status symbol was to hire identical twins as footmen, resembling a pair of book-ends.

THE SIGHT OF THIS FOOTMAN AND HIS AMPLE CALVES IS CERTAINLY A CAUSE OF AMUSEMENT TO THE RAGAMUFFIN BEHIND HIM.

DRESS

The footman in livery only finds himself in stockings, shoes, and washing. Where silk stockings, or extra articles of linen are worn, they are provided by the family, as well as his livery, a working dress, consisting of a pair of overalls, a waistcoat, a fustian jacket, with a white or jean one for times when he is liable to be called to answer the door or wait at breakfast; and, on quitting his service, he is expected to leave behind him any livery had within six months.

THREE FOOTMEN,
IMMACULATELY
DRESSED IN A
TYPICAL LIVERY
OF DARK
TAILCOAT AND
BLACK BREECHES.

[*82*]

Hippolyte Taine describes 'the footmen in great houses with white cravats impeccably tied, scarlet or canary yellow breeches, magnificent dimensions and proportions; their calves, especially, are enormous... in great houses they are carefully matched: the footmen, like a pair of carriage horses, must be exactly the same size... fullness of calves, ankles, nobility of bearing, decorative appearance, all may be worth an extra £20.00 per annum'. This was on top of the usual £30.00 a year wage. The footman also supplemented his salary with tips and other gifts from the mistress of the house and appreciative guests. A pair of matching footmen were the showpiece of the household to the outside world when they escorted their employers in their carriage, or escorted the mistress shopping, carrying her parcels but always walking several paces behind.

The Footman

A FOOTMAN
BEARING
THE TEA TRAY
TO HIS
EMPLOYERS.

DUTIES OF THE FOOTMAN

Where a single footman, or odd man, is the only male servant, then, whatever his ostensible position, he is required to make himself generally useful. He has to clean the knives and forks, the shoes, the furniture, the plate; answer the visitors who call, the drawing-room and parlour bells; and do all errands. His life is no sinecure; and a methodical arrangement of his time will be necessary, in order to perform his many duties with any satisfaction to himself or his master.

He has many of the duties of the upper servants to perform as

THE MISTRESS, GIVING HER FOOT-MAN HIS ORDERS FOR THE DAY.

well as his own, and more constant occupation; he will also have the arrangement of his time more immediately under his own control, and he will do well to reduce it to a methodical division. All his rough work should be done before breakfast is ready, when he must appear clean and in a presentable state. After breakfast, when everything belonging to his pantry is cleaned and put in its place, the furniture in the dining and drawing rooms requires rubbing. Towards noon, the parlour luncheon is to be prepared; and he must be at his mistress's disposal to go out with the carriage, or follow her if she walks out.

When required to go out with the carriage, it is the footman's duty to see that it has come to the door perfectly clean, and that the glasses, and sashes, and linings, are free from dust. In receiving messages at the carriage door, he should turn his ear to the speaker, so as to comprehend what is said, in order that he may give directions to the coachman clearly. In closing the door upon the family, he should see that the handle is securely turned, and that no part of the ladies' dress is shut in. When the house he is to call on is reached, he should knock and return to the carriage for orders.

Although a footman did a variety of work in the house there is seldom any reference to him carrying the coals or carting the heavy water buckets upstairs. These jobs seem to have been left to the female domestics. A first footman with ambition would work hard and learn all he could from the butler, eventually moving up the domestic ladder to become one himself. So it was with the second, or junior footman, who acted as an apprentice to the senior footman.

SALVERS, LIKE THIS ONE, WERE OFTEN USED BY FOOTMEN FOR PRESENTING VISITING CARDS AND OTHER ITEMS TO THE MASTER.

The footman is expected to rise early, in order to get through all his dirty work before the family are stirring. Boots and shoes, and knives and forks, should be cleaned, lamps in use trimmed, his master's clothes brushed, the furniture rubbed over; so that he may put aside his working dress, tidy himself, and appear in a clean jean jacket to lay the cloth and prepare breakfast for the family.

He lays the cloth on the table; over the breakfast-cloth, and sets the breakfast things in order, and then proceeds to wait upon his master, if he has any of the duties of a valet to perform.

In grand establishments there were often up to eight or ten footmen, with some acting as special attendants or valets to the young adult sons of the family. In smaller houses there might have been only one male servant and he would have a great deal of work to get through each day with not much time left for looking glamorous. Where there were no servant's quarters, most of the male staff slept downstairs, often in cramped, damp basements with very little comfort or amenities.

MISHAPS SUCH AS THIS WERE TO BE AVOIDED AT ALL COSTS. SERVANTS WERE ALWAYS SUPPOSED TO BE DISCREET AND QUIET IN THEIR MOVEMENTS.

Where a valet is not kept, a portion of his duties falls to the footman, brushing the clothes among others. When the hat is silk, it requires brushing every day with a soft brush; after rain, it requires wiping the way of the nap before drying, and when nearly dry, brushing with a soft brush and with the hat-stick in it. If the footman is required to perform any part of a valet's duties, he will have to see that the housemaid lights a fire in the dressing-room in due time; that the room is dusted and cleaned; that the washhand-ewer is filled with soft water; and that the bath, whether hot or cold, is ready when required; that towels are at hand; that hair-brushes and combs are properly cleansed, and in their places; that hot water is ready at the hour ordered; the dressing-gown and slippers in their place, the clean linen aired, and the clothes to be worn for the day in their proper places. After the master has dressed, it will be the footman's duty to restore

everything to its place properly cleansed and dry, and the whole restored to order.

At breakfast, when there is no butler, the footman carries up the tea-urn, and, assisted by the housemaid, he waits during breakfast. Breakfast over, he removes the tray and other things off the table, folds up the breakfast-cloth, and sets the room in order, by sweeping up all crumbs, shaking the cloth, and laying it on the table again, making up the fire, and sweeping up the hearth.

At luncheon-time nearly the same routine is observed, except where the footman is either out with the carriage or away on other business, when in the absence of any butler, the housemaid must assist.

SERVING TEA

As soon as the drawing-room bell rings for tea, the footman enters with the tray, which has been previously prepared; hands the tray round to the company, with cream and sugar, the tea and coffee being generally poured out, while another attendant hands cakes, toast, or biscuits. If it is an ordinary family party, where this social meal is prepared by the mistress, he carries the urn or kettle, as the case may be; hands around the toast, or such other eatable as may be required, removing the whole in the same manner when tea is over.

DINNER

For dinner, the footman lays the cloth, taking care that the table is not too near the fire, if there is one, and that passage-room is left. A tablecloth should be laid without a wrinkle; and this requires two persons: over this the slips are laid, which are usually removed preparatory to placing dessert on the table. He prepares knives and forks, and glasses, with five or six plates for each person. This done, he places chairs enough for the party, distributing them equally on each side of the table, and opposite to each a napkin neatly folded, within it a piece of bread or small roll, and a knife and fork on the right side of each plate, a fork on the left, and a carving-knife and fork at the top and bottom of the table, outside the others, with the rests opposite to them, and a gravy-spoon beside the knife. The fish-slice should be at the top, where the lady of the house, with the assistance of the gentleman next to her, divides the fish, and the soup-ladle at the bottom: it is sometimes usual to add a dessert-knife and fork; at the same time, on the right side also, of each plate, put a wine-glass for as many kinds of wine as it is intended to hand around, and a finger-glass or glass-cooler about four inches from the edge. The latter are frequently put on the table with the dessert. Salt-cellars should be placed on the table in number sufficient for the guests, so that each may help themselves, or, at least, their immediate neighbours.

About half an hour before dinner, he rings the dinner-bell, where that is the practice, and occupies himself with carrying up everything he is likely to require. At the expiration of the time, having communicated with the cook, he rings the dinner-bell, and proceeds to take it up, with such assistance as he can obtain. Having ascertained that all is in order, that his own dress is clean and presentable, and his white cotton gloves are without a stain, he announces in the drawing-room that dinner is served, and stands respectfully by the door until the company are seated: he places himself on the left, behind his master, who is to distribute the soup; where soup and fish are served together, his place will be at his mistress's left hand; but he must be on the alert to see that whoever is assisting him, whether male or female, are at their posts.

VISITING SERVANTS

If any of the guests has brought his own servant with him, his place is behind his master's chair, rendering such assistance to others as he can, while attending to his master's wants throughout the dinner, so that every guest has what he requires. This necessitates both activity and intelligence, and should be done without bustle, without asking any questions, except where it is the custom of the house to hand around dishes or wine, when it will be necessary to mention, in a quiet or unobtrusive manner, the dish or wine you present.

At the end of the first course, notice is conveyed to the cook, who is waiting to send up the second, which is introduced in the same way as before; the attendants who remove the fragments, carrying the dishes from the kitchen, and handing them to the footman or butler, whose duty it is to arrange them on the table. After dinner, the dessert-glasses and wines are placed on the table by the footman, who places himself behind his master's chair, to supply wine and hand round the ices and other refreshments, all other servants leaving the room.

While attentive to all, the footman should be obtrusive to none; he should give nothing but on a waiter, and always hand it with the left hand and on the left side of the person he serves, and hold it so that the guest may take it with ease. In lifting dishes from the table, he should use both hands, and remove them with care, so that nothing is spilt on the table-cloth or on the dresses of the guests.

During dinner each person's knife, fork, plate, and spoon should be changed as soon as he has done with it; the vegetables and sauces belonging to the different dishes presented without remark to the guests; and the footman should tread lightly moving round, and, if possible, should bear in mind, if there is a wit or humorist of the party, whose good things keep the table in a roar, they are not expected to reach his ears.

After each meal, the footman's place is in his pantry: here perfect order should prevail–a place for everything and everything in its place. A sink, with hot and cold water laid on, is very desirable–cold absolutely necessary. Wooden bowls or tubs of sufficient capacity are required, one for hot and another for cold water. Have the bowl three parts full of clean hot water; in this wash all plate and plated articles which are greasy, wiping them before cleaning with a brush.

It is the footman's duty to carry messages or letters for his master or mistress to their friends, to the post, or to the tradespeople; and nothing is more important than dispatch and exactness in doing so, although writing even the simplest message is now the ordinary and very proper practice. Dean Swift, among his other quaint directions, recommends a perusal of all such epistles, in order that you may be more able to fulfil your duty to your master. Politeness and civility to visitors is one of the things masters and mistresses have a right to expect, and should exact rigorously.

A FOOTMAN WAS OFTEN REQUIRED TO CARRY MESSAGES FOR HIS EMPLOYERS.

When visitors present themselves, the servant charged with the duty of opening the door will open it promptly, and answer, without hesitation, if the family are "not at home", or "engaged;" which generally means the same thing, and might be oftener used with advantage to morals. On the contrary, if he has no such orders, he will answer affirmatively, open the door wide to admit them, and precede them to open the door of the drawing-room. If the family are not there, he will place chairs for them, open the blinds (if the room is too dark), and intimate civilly that he goes to inform his mistress. If the lady is in her drawing-room, he announces the name of the visitors, having previously acquainted himself with it. In this part of his duty it is necessary to be very careful to repeat the names correctly; mispronouncing names is very apt to give offence, and leads sometimes to other disagreeables. The writer was once initiated into some of the secrets on the "other side" of a legal affair in which he took an interest, before he could correct a mistake made by the servant in announcing him. When the

visitor is departing, the servant should be at hand, ready, when rung for, to open the door; he should open it with a respectful manner, and close it gently when the visitors are fairly beyond the threshold. When several visitors arrive together, he should take care not to mix up the different names together, where they belong to the same family, as Mr., Mrs., and Miss.; if they are strangers, he should announce each as distinctly as possible.

Masters as well as servants sometimes make mistakes; but it is not expected that a servant will correct any omissions, even if he should have time to notice them, although with the best intentions: thus it would not be correct, for instance, if he observed that his master took wine with the ladies all round, as some gentlemen still continue to do, but stopped at some one: to nudge him on the shoulder and say, as was done by the servant of a Scottish gentleman, "What ails you at her in the green grown?" It will be better to leave the lady unnoticed than for the servant to turn his master into ridicule.

RECEPTIONS
AND EVENING PARTIES

The drawing-rooms being prepared, the card-tables laid out with cards and counters, and such other arrangements as are necessary made for the reception of the company, the rooms should be lighted up as the hour appointed approaches. Attendants in the drawing-room, even more than the dining-room, should move about actively but noiselessly: no creaking of shoes, which is an abomination; watching the lights from time to time, so as to keep up their brilliancy. But even if the attendant likes a game of cribbage or whist himself, he must not interfere in his master or mistress's game, nor even seem to take an interest in it.

FOOTMEN WERE
SOMETHING OF
A STATUS SYMBOL
AND MORE HIGHLY
PAID THAN MOST
FEMALE SERVANTS.
A GOOD FOOTMAN
MIGHT ASPIRE
TO BECOMING
A BUTLER.

[*93*]

Dine we must, well dine elegar wholesomely...

d we may as

ly as well as

THE DINING ROOM

M AN, IT IS SAID, is a dining animal. Creatures of the inferior races eat and drink; only man dines. The nation which knows how to dine has learnt the leading lesson of progress. It implies both the will and the skill to reduce to order, and surround with idealisms and graces, the more material conditions of human existence; and wherever that will and that skill exist, life cannot be wholly ignoble.

Second only to the drawing room in importance and as a means of establishing the wealth and position of the owners of the house, was the dining room. Most dining rooms in the Victorian era contained a large dining table, seating from 12 to as many as 20 guests. The table was usually of solid dark mahogany, as were the chairs. Red or crimson flock wallpaper, in floral or arabesque patterns, covered the walls and chairs were upholstered in the same colour tones. The windows were heavily draped, not only for warmth in winter, but also to keep out dust and soot.

A most important feature was a mirror above the mantle. The cognoscenti of the time recommended that this should be higher than it was wide, while still extending across the full width of the mantle. Another feature was the sideboard, which was at times groaning with elaborate dishes of food or made an ideal place on which to display more ornamentation. If the sideboard was of a pedestal design there

GUESTS ENTERED
THE DINING ROOM
IN STRICT ORDER
OF RANK AND
IMPORTANCE.
THE HOST
ESCORTED THE
HIGHEST-RANKING
FEMALE GUEST.

TABLES WERE
LAID WITH THE
UTMOST CARE AND
ATTENTION TO
DETAIL.

would often be a wine cooler on the floor in the centre, which would house ice to keep the wine cool during the evening.

Ideally there would be a second smaller sideboard or chiffonier on another wall, laden with yet more possessions as a show of wealth to impress the guests. Displaying one's material wealth was very important to the Victorians and the more objects they could display the more it proved their place in 'polite society'.

There may also have been a dumb waiter or side table, again in dark mahogany, with three tiers of shelving for displaying the dessert as well as the plate, glasses and other articles used during the meal. These pieces of furniture were set on castors making it easy to move about the room if necessary and for wheeling away used articles. Great store was set on the presentation of the table, the immaculate, freshly

[*98*]

pressed cloth and napkins, the spotless cutlery, the correct placing of patterned crockery, shining silver condiment containers and many other adornments. In grand establishments, the layout of the cutlery was of paramount importance and it was known for the host or hostess to enter the dining room prior to dinner with a tape measure to check the dimensions were exact.

Central floral arrangements were to be low enough so as not to obstruct the view of the opposite diner and not so heavily perfumed as to overpower one's senses. The temperature of the room was another consideration. If there was a blazing fire it could be unbearably hot by the end of the meal for the gentlemen, but if there was no fire, the ladies could suffer from the cold in their fancy dinner dresses.

Lighting also needed to be attended to before the guests entered the dining room. Candlesticks were most often used, but

enough light was needed to enable the servants to go about their duties while not having direct light in the faces of the guests.

There were definite rules on etiquette. If a guest was new to the grand table settings and the dos and don'ts of a high-class establishment, they could find themselves in embarrassing situations. The rule to remember was, if not sure what to do, watch your neighbours in the hope that they know the correct procedure.

CRUET STANDS
WERE ELABORATE
AND OFTEN
SILVER OR SILVER-
PLATED.

MRS BEETON
ADVISED THAT
FLORAL ARRANGE-
MENTS FOR THE
TABLE SHOULD BE
KEPT LOW ENOUGH
FOR GUESTS TO SEE
THOSE OPPOSITE
THEM WITH EASE.

The half-hour before dinner has always been considered as a great ordeal through which the mistress, in giving a dinner-party, will either pass with flying colours, or lose many of her laurels. The anxiety to receive her guests, — her hope that all will be present in due time, — her trust in the skill of her cook, and the attention of the other domestics, all tend to make these few minutes a trying time. The mistress, however, must display no kind of agitation, but show her tact in suggesting light and cheerful subjects of conversation, which will be much aided by the introduction of any particularly new book, curiosity of art, or article of vertu, which may pleasantly engage the attention of the company.

In giving an entertainment of this kind, the mistress should remember that it is her duty to make her guests feel happy, comfortable, and quite at their ease; and the guests should also consider that they have come to the house of their hostess to be happy. Thus an opportunity is given to all for innocent enjoyment and intellectual improvement, when also acquaintances may be formed that may prove invaluable through life, and information gained that will enlarge the mind.

Such were the trials and tribulations of the lady of the house before a formal dinner party, and the success of the evening could mar or make the standing of the family in society.

A SELECTION OF CHINA, INCLUDING DINNER AND DESSERT PLATES, VEGETABLE DISHES AND A SOUP TUREEN.

PRESENTATION OF THE TABLE

Dinner, being the grand solid meal of the day, is a matter of considerable importance; and a well-served table is a striking index of human ingenuity and resource.

The decorations of the table vary at different seasons: the vase of flowers of daily use, is on occasions replaced by plants in full bloom, or by small fruit-trees laden with their rich burden—for instance, in early spring, strawberry plants in full fruit should grace the centre of the table, cherry trees succeed, and are followed by apple, pear, apricot and plum trees in succession, trained vines appear later, and orange trees adorn the 'mid-winter' mahogany. These trees are pretty and fashionable, and should be placed in elegant pots, of which the Pompeian patterns and colours should be selected, as relieving the monotonous brilliancy of the white table-cloth.

Still more *à la mode* is to adorn the centre of the table with trays of varied form, the trays being concealed beneath a mass of flowers; the flowers are kept as low as possible, in imitation of parterre gardening. These trays of flowers have entirely superseded the high epergne, which is certainly very elegant, but which possesses the disadvantage of entirely shutting out those who face it from the view of their opposite neighbours.

We consider that the low trays are a great improvement: they are made in silver and electro-plate, and are fitted with glass; Japanese trays, which are now very reasonable in price, answer every purpose of this kind of table decoration.

According to what is to be served so must the table be laid, but there are certain rules that apply equally to all. Everything necessary for laying the cloth should first be brought into the room and the serviettes be ready folded, and it is a good plan to put these round first, so that the same amount of space can be allowed to each person. These occupy the space between the knives and forks, and in each should be put a dinner roll or a piece of bread cut rather thick. The water carafes and salt cellars may next be laid. Of the former there should be at any rate one at each corner of the table,

MRS BEETON
RECOMMENDS
FERNS AS TABLE
DECORATIONS.
PLANTS IN LARGE,
LOW CONTAINERS
LIKE THIS ONE
WERE SUITABLE
FOR USE AS
A CENTREPIECE.
OPPOSITE IS
A MORE ELABORATE
FLOWER VASE.

2997. *The Palm Leaf.*

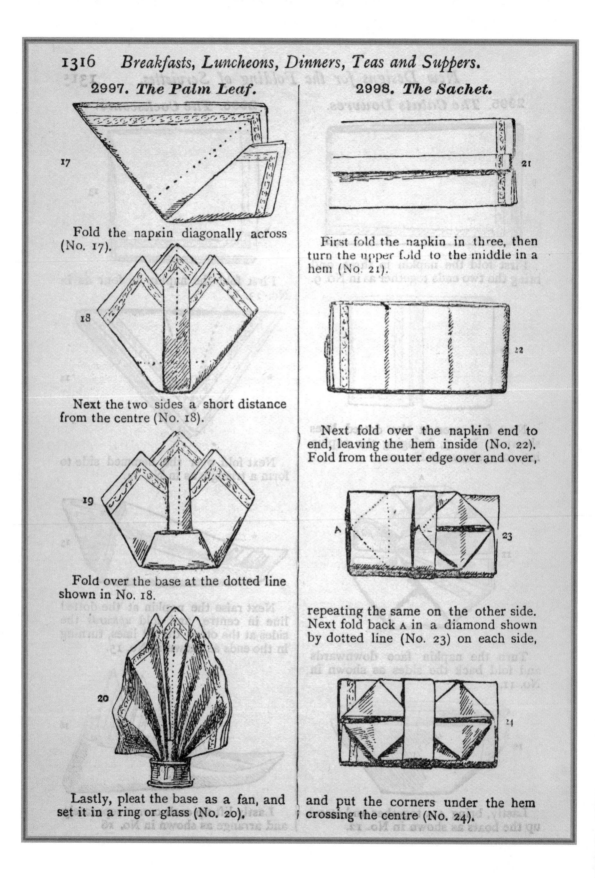

Fold the napkin diagonally across (No. 17).

Next the two sides a short distance from the centre (No. 18).

Fold over the base at the dotted line shown in No. 18.

Lastly, pleat the base as a fan, and set it in a ring or glass (No. 20).

2998. *The Sachet.*

First fold the napkin in three, then turn the upper fold to the middle in a hem (No. 21).

Next fold over the napkin end to end, leaving the hem inside (No. 22). Fold from the outer edge over and over, repeating the same on the other side. Next fold back A in a diamond shown by dotted line (No. 23) on each side, and put the corners under the hem crossing the centre (No. 24).

while there should be a salt cellar between every two persons. Unless silver salt cellars are used, the glass ones should match the rest of the service. Now we come to the knives and forks, and of these it is usual to lay two large of each, flanked to the right by a fish knife and a soup spoon, and on the left by the fish fork; other knives and forks are supplied with the plates for the different courses

The question of what wine is to be drunk at dinner will determine what glasses will be wanted, as the glasses used for dessert are put on afterwards. Supposing, as is so often the case, sherry, champagne and claret are to be served, put the proper glasses for each to the right side of each person, setting them in a triangle, with the sherry glass (the first used) at the top, just reaching to the point of the knife, but at a convenient distance from it.

Many middle-class Victorians added fish knives and forks to their canteen of cutlery. These may have been fashionable in some circles, but in others it showed that these pretentious additions were not even of Georgian silver and had been newly bought, not inherited.

AS MRS BEETON SAYS: 'THE ELEGANCE WITH WHICH A DINNER IS SERVED IS A MATTER WHICH DEPENDS PARTLY UPON THE MEANS, BUT STILL MORE UPON THE TASTE OF THE MASTER AND MISTRESS OF THE HOUSE'— HENCE THE GREAT IMPORTANCE OF A WELL FURNISHED DINING ROOM.

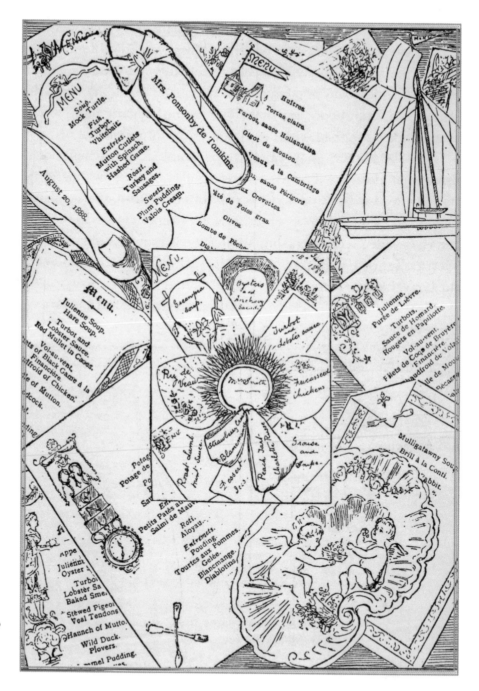

DINNER MENU
CARDS COULD BE
WRITTEN BY HAND
OR SPECIALLY
PRINTED FOR THE
OCCASION.

DINNER-PARTIES

Cards, or invitations for a dinner-party, should be issued a fortnight or three weeks (sometimes even a month) beforehand, and care should be taken by the hostess, in the selection of the invited guests, that they should be suited to each other.

It will be found of great assistance to the placing of a party at the dinner-table to have the names of the guests neatly (and correctly) written on small cards, and placed at that part of the table where it is desired they should sit.

With respect to the number of guests, it has often been said, that a private dinner-party should consist of not less than the number of the Graces, or more than that of the Muses. A party of ten or twelve is, perhaps, in a general way, sufficient to enjoy themselves and be enjoyed.

Kid gloves are worn by ladies at dinner-parties, but should be taken off before the business of dining commences.

The elegance with which a modern dinner is served is a matter which depends, of course, partly upon the means, but still more upon the taste of the master and mistress of the house. Much also of the pleasure of a dinner-party will depend on the arrangement of the guests at table, so as to form a due ad-mixture of talkers and listeners, the grave and the gay.

Many celebrated men and women have been great talkers; and, amongst others, the genial Sir Walter Scott, who spoke freely to every one, and a favourite remark of whom it was, that he never did so without learning something he didn't know before.

It may be observed, in passing, that the poets, though they have more to say about wine than solid food, because the former more directly stimulates the intellect and the feelings, do not flinch from the subject of eating and drinking.

[*107*]

DINNER FOR 12 PERSONS (SEPTEMBER)

FIRST COURSE.

*Mock–Turtle Soup.
Soup à la Jardinière.
Salmon and Lobster Sauce.
Fried Whitings.
Stewed Eels.*

—

ENTRÉES.

*Veal Cutlets.
Scalloped Oysters.
Curried Fowl.
Grilled Mushrooms.*

—

SECOND COURSE.

*Haunch of Mutton.
Boiled Calf's Head à la Béchamel.
Braised Ham.
Roast Fowls aux Cressons.*

THIRD COURSE.

*Leveret.
Grouse.
Cabinet Pudding.
Iced Pudding.
Compôte of Plumbs.
Damson Tart.
Cream.
Fruit Jelly.
Prawns.
Lobster Salad.*

—

DESSERTS AND ICES.

CURTAINS WERE
OFTEN KEPT
DRAWN, EVEN IN
THE DAYTIME.
THE VICTORIANS
CONSIDERED
SUNLIGHT BAD FOR
BOTH FURNITURE
AND PEOPLE.

Dinner being announced, the host offers his arm to, and places on his right hand at the dinner-table, the lady to whom he desires to pay most respect, either on account of her age, position, or from her being the greatest stranger in the party. If this lady be married and her husband present, the latter takes the hostess — who always enters the dining-room last—to her place at table, and seats himself at her right hand. The rest of the company follow the host in couples, as specified by the master or mistress of the house, the whole party being arranged according to their rank and other circumstances which may be known to the hostess.

The guests being seated at the dinner-table, the lady begins to help the soup, which is handed round, commencing with the gentleman on her right and on her left, and continuing in the same order till all are served. It is generally established as a rule, not to ask for soup or fish twice, as, in so doing, part of the company may be kept waiting too long for the second course, when, perhaps, a little revenge is taken by looking at the awkward consumer of a second portion. This rule, however, may, under various circumstances, not be considered as absolutely binding.

It is not usual, where taking wine is *en règle*, for a gentleman to ask a lady to take wine until the fish or soup is finished, and when the gentleman honoured by sitting on the right of the hostess may politely inquire if she will do him the honour of taking wine with him. This will act as a signal to the rest of the company, the gentleman of the house most probably requesting the same pleasure

A SOUP TUREEN, PLATES AND LADLE. SOUP WAS NEARLY ALWAYS PART OF THE FIRST COURSE OF A DINNER MENU.

DINNER PARTY
GUESTS TAKE
THEIR SEATS AT
THE TABLE.

of the ladies at his right and left. At many tables, however, the custom or fashion of drinking wine in this manner is abolished, and the servant fills the glasses of the guests with the various wines suited to the course which is in progress.

When dinner is finished, the dessert is placed on the table, accompanied by finger-glasses. It is the custom of some gentleman to wet a corner of the napkin; but the hostess, whose behaviour will set the tone to all the ladies present, will merely wet the tips of her fingers, which will serve all the purposes required. The French and other continentals have a habit of gargling the mouth; but it is a custom which no English gentlewoman should in the slightest degree imitate.

PLAIN FAMILY DINNERS FOR JULY

SUNDAY.—1. *Julienne soup.
2. Roast lamb, half calf's head,
tongue and brains, boiled ham,
peas and potatoes.
3. Cherry tart, custards.*

———

MONDAY.—1. *Hashed calf's head,
cold lamb and salad. 2. Vegetable
marrow and white sauce,
instead of pudding.*

———

TUESDAY.—1. *Stewed veal, with
peas, young carrots, and potatoes.
Small meat pie. 2. Raspberry-
and-currant pudding.*

———

WEDNESDAY.—1. *Roast ducks
stuffed, gravy, peas, and potatoes; the
remains of stewed veal rechauffé.
2. Macaroni served as a
sweet pudding.*

THURSDAY.—1. *Slices of salmon
and caper sauce. 2. Boiled knuckle of
veal, parsley-and-butter, vegetable
marrow and potatoes.
3. Black-currant pudding.*

———

FRIDAY.—1. *Roast shoulder
of mutton, onion sauce, peas
and potatoes. 2. Cherry tart,
baked custard pudding.*

———

SATURDAY.—1. *Minced mutton,
Rump-steak-and-kidney pudding.
2. Baked lemon pudding.*

When fruit has been taken, and a glass or two of wine passed round, the time will arrive when the hostess will rise, and thus give the signal for the ladies to leave the gentlemen, and retire to the drawing-room. The gentlemen of the party will rise at the same time, and he who is nearest the door will open it for the ladies, all remaining courteously standing until the last lady has withdrawn.

In former times, when the bottle circulated freely amongst the guests, it was necessary for the ladies to retire earlier than they do at present, for the gentlemen of the company soon became unfit to conduct themselves with that decorum which is essential in the presence of ladies. Delicacy of conduct towards the female sex has increased with the esteem in which they are now universally held, and, thus, the very early withdrawal of the ladies from the dining-room is to be deprecated. A lull in the conversation will seasonably indicate the moment for the ladies' departure.

Once the ladies retired from the dining room, port and brandy would be passed around the table, occasionally with an accompaniment of 'zests' (food having a spicy, piquant flavour), such as anchovy toast and Welsh rarebit. These offerings were considered too highly spiced to be offered to the ladies.

THE FOOD

Dine we must, and we may as well dine elegantly as well as wholesomely.

It has been said, indeed, that great men, in general, are great diners. This, however, can scarcely be true of any great men but men of action; and in that case, it would simply imply that persons of vigorous constitution, who work hard, eat heartily; for, of course, a life of action requires a vigorous constitution.

A SELECTION OF
SUPPER DISHES,
TYPICAL OF THE
ELABORATE MENUS
SUGGESTED BY
MRS BEETON.

Roast Fowl.

Pheasant.

Game Pie with Jelly.

Shrimp Patties.

Oyster Patties.

Lobster Salad.

Savoury Jelly a la Bellevue.

Brawn.

Pigeon Pie

Galantine of Veal.

Russian Salad.

Crayfish.

Ham Garnished.

Tongue Garnished.

EVEN AT WHAT
MRS BEETON
DESCRIBES AS
A 'PLAIN FAMILY
SUPPER' THREE
HEARTY COURSES
WERE SERVED.

Leaving great men of all kinds, however, to get their own dinners, let us, who are not great, look after ours.

The great variety in the dishes which furnish a modern dinner-table, does not necessarily imply anything unwholesome, or anything capricious.

Food that is not well relished cannot be digested; and the appetite of the over-worked man of business, or statesman, or of any dweller in towns, whose occupations are exciting and exhausting, is jaded, and requires stimulation.

A great gastronomist has some aphorisms and short directions in relation to dinner-parties, which are well deserving of notice:– "Let the dishes be few in number in the first course, but proportionally good. The order of the food is from the most substantial to the lightest. The order of drinking wine is from the mildest to the most foamy and most perfumed. To invite a person to your house is to take charge of his happiness so long as he is beneath your roof. The mistress of the house should always be certain that the coffee be excellent; whilst the master should be answerable for the quality of his wines and liqueurs."

The order of the courses should be as follows, when placed upon the table:– The First Course usually soup, then fish, then come the entrées (made dishes). The next Course joints, poultry, &c, and after these, game and savoury dishes, then sweets, then cheese, cooked or uncooked, or such small savouries as anchovy toast. When there are roast meats they would be opposite colours, thus, not two whites or browns. Place joints upon large dishes, as they form a considerable portion of the dinner. Entrées require care in handling, there is nearly always gravy with them, and this must not be upset upon the cloth. The Third Course used to be entrées, joints, poultry, &c and removes. Next in order came the creams, pastry, and sweets; this way The Fourth Course and fifth consisted of cheese, butter, celery, salads, &c. The last arrangement of dishes — which cannot be called a course, seeing that the dinner is virtually over — the dessert, this comprising tastefully-arranged fruits that are most in season, together with appropriate dried fruits that are seasonable all year round.

A SIDEBOARD WAS AN ESSENTIAL PIECE OF DINING ROOM FURNITURE, USED FOR DISPLAYING CHINA AND SILVER.

Now the soup is very often preceded by such little dishes as caviar, croutons, oysters, and other little appetisans, while others are introduced during the meal, and every dish forms a separate course.

BILL OF FARE FOR A PICNIC FOR 40 PERSONS

*A joint of cold roast beef, a joint of
cold boiled beef, 2 ribs of lamb,
2 shoulders of lamb, 4 roast fowls,
2 roast ducks, 1 ham, 1 tongue, 2 veal-
and-ham pies, 2 pigeon pies,
6 medium-sized lobsters, 1 piece of
collared calf's head, 18 lettuces,
6 baskets of salad, 6 cucumbers.*

———

*Stewed fruit well sweetened, and
put into glass bottles well corked;
3 or 4 dozen plain pastry biscuits
to eat with the stewed fruit,
2 dozen fruit turnovers, 4 dozen
cheesecakes, 2 cold cabinet puddings
in moulds, 2 blancmanges in moulds, a
few jam puffs, 1 large cold plum-
pudding (this must be good), a few
baskets of fresh fruit, 3 dozen plain
biscuits, a piece of cheese, 6 lbs. of
butter (this, of course, includes the
butter for tea), 4 quartern loaves
of household broad, 3 dozen rolls,
6 loaves of tin bread (for tea), 2 plain
plum cakes, 2 pound cakes, 2 sponge
cakes, a tin of mixed biscuits, ½ lb. of
tea. Coffee is not suitable for a picnic,
being difficult to make.*

THINGS NOT TO BE FORGOTTEN
AT A PICNIC. A stick of horse-
radish, a bottle of mint-sauce well
corked, a bottle of salad dressing, a
bottle of vinegar, made mustard,
pepper, salt, good oil, and pounded
sugar. If it can be managed, take a
little ice. It is scarcely necessary to
say that plates, tumblers, wine-
glasses, knives, forks, and spoons,
must not be forgotten; as also tea-
cups and saucers, 3 or 4 teapots,
some lump sugar, and milk, if this
last-named article cannot be obtained in the neighbourhood. Take
3 corkscrews.

BEVERAGES.—*3 dozen quart bottles
of ale, packed in hampers; ginger-beer,
soda-water, and lemonade, of each
2 dozen bottles; 6 bottles of sherry,
6 bottles of claret, champagne à
discrétion, and any other light wine
that may be preferred, and 2 bottles
of brandy. Water can usually be
obtained so it is useless to take it.*

À LA RUSSE

———

A SELECTION OF
DISHES MRS
BEETON SUGGESTS
AS SUITABLE
FOR SERVING AT
A SUPPER FOR
TEN TO TWELVE
PERSONS.

Le Diner à la Russe, introduced into this country some years since
has been received with various degrees of satisfaction and encouragement. Some mistresses have attempted it, and have relinquished
the plan; others have considered it a success, and maintain the style.
It is impossible to decide, absolutely whether the old style or the

AT A DINNER À LA
RUSSE, DISHES
WERE CARVED
AWAY FROM
THE TABLE AND
EACH PERSON
WAS SERVED
HIS OR HER
OWN PORTION.

new is the better, because many conditions govern the verdict. But we may at this point say, that for a household which is not very well appointed, and has not ample space and resources, it is not a kind of entertainment likely to be attended by any great *éclat*.

At dinners *à la russe*, flowers occupy with the dessert the whole space unoccupied by the plates of the convives. In the real Russian banquet, the table is extremely narrow, the ladies all walk in together and are followed by the gentlemen, who sit opposite them, the servants come and hand round every dish, the vegetables are served in separate compartments of a large round dish. When the dessert is handed round, the guests help themselves to all they are likely to require at once; the dessert is replaced upon the table and not again touched. On retiring from table, the ladies again precede the gentlemen, and all take their departure at once, unless invited especially to spend the evening: a custom that might be followed with advantage at many reunions out of Russia.

SERVICE À LA RUSSE (JULY)

Juliènne Soup.
Vermicelli Soup.

—

Boiled Salmon.
Turbot and Lobster Sauce.

—

Soles–Water Souchy.
Perch–Water Souchy.

—

Matelote d'Anguilles à la Toulouse.
Filets de Soles à la Normandie.

—

Red Mullet.
Trout.

—

Lobster Rissoles.
Whitebait.

—

Riz de Veau à la Banquière.
Filets de Poulets aux Coucombres.

—

Canards à la Rouennaise.
Mutton Cutlets à la Jardinière.

—

Braised Beef à la Flamande.
Spring Chickens.

Roast Quarter of Lamb.
Roast Saddle of Mutton.

—

Tongue.
Ham and Peas.

—

Quails, larded.
Roast Ducks.
Turkey Poult, larded.

—

Mayonnaise of Chicken.
Tomatas.
Green Peas à la Française.

—

Suédoise of Strawberries.
Charlotte Russe.
Compôte of Cherries.

—

Neapolitan Cakes.
Pastry.
Madeira Wine Jelly.

—

Iced Pudding à la Nesselrode.

DESSERT AND ICES.

NOTE.—Dinners *à la Russe* differ from ordinary dinners in the mode of serving the various dishes. In a dinner à la Russe, the dishes are cut up on a sideboard, and handed round to the guests, and each dish may be considered a course. The table for a dinner *à la Russe* should be laid with flowers and plants in fancy flowerpots down the middle, together with some of the dessert dishes. A menu or bill of fare should be laid by the side of each guest.

Dinners *à la Russe* are scarcely suitable for small establishments; a large number of servants being required to carve; and to help the guests; besides there being a necessity for more plates, dishes, knives, forks, and spoons, than are usually to be found in any other than a very large establishment. Where, however, a service *à la Russe* is practicable, there is, perhaps, no mode of serving a dinner so enjoyable as this.

The influence o
immense upon
of a household.

the cook is

he happiness

THE COOK

IN THE LARGER establishments of the Middle Ages, cooks, with the authority of feudal chiefs, gave their orders from a high chair in which they ensconced themselves, and commanded a view of all that was going on throughout their several domains. Each held a long wooden spoon, with which he tasted, without leaving his seat, the various comestibles that were cooking on the stoves, and which he frequently used as a rod of punishment on the backs of those whose idleness and gluttony too largely predominated over their diligence and temperance.

As in the fine arts the progress of mankind from barbarism to civilization is marked by a gradual succession of triumphs over the rude materialities of nature, so in the Art of Cookery is the progress gradual. From the earliest and simplest modes, to those of the most complicated and refined. Accordingly, the art of cookery commences; and although the fruits of the earth, the fowls of the air, the beasts of the field, and the fish of the sea, are still the only food of mankind, yet these are so prepared, improved, and dressed by skill and ingenuity, that they are the means of immeasurably extending the boundaries of human enjoyments.

Everything that is edible, and passes under the hands of the

cook, is more or less changed, and assumes new forms. Hence the influence of that functionary is immense upon the happiness of a household.

Many cooks began their working life as scullery- or kitchen-maids and, if they were ambitious and hard-working young girls, they would learn all they could from the resident cook. This way they gradually moved up the ladder until they were skilled enough to become an under-cook or an apprentice to the chef and then move on to being employed as a full-time cook. This would take several years and most cooks were of a mature age when they finished their training. They were always known to the family as 'cook' and to the other servants as 'Mrs'. They were often widows who had cooked for their own family, but whether married or not they were always 'Mrs'.

In the luxurious ages of Grecian antiquity, Sicilian cooks were the most esteemed, and received high awards for their services. Among them, one called Trimalcio was such an adept in his art, that he could impart to common fish both the form and flavour of the most esteemed of the piscatory tribes. A chief cook in the palmy days of Roman voluptuousness had about £800 a year, and Antony rewarded the one that cooked the supper which pleased Cleopatra, with the present of a city. With the fall of the Empire, the culinary art sank into less consideration. In the Middle Ages, cooks laboured to acquire a reputation for their sauces, which they composed of strange combinations, for the sake of novelty, as well as singularity.

COOK PREPARING
CURDS AND
WHEY—MILK
SEPARATED INTO
SOLIDS AND
LIQUID WHICH
WAS SOMETIMES
GIVEN TO
CHILDREN AS
A PUDDING.

Excellence in the art of cookery, as in all other things, is only attainable by practice and experience. In proportion therefore, to the opportunities

which a cook has had of these, so will be his excellence in the art. It is in the establishments of princes, noblemen, and very affluent families alone, that the man-cook is found in this country. He, therefore, holds a high position in a household, being inferior in rank, only to the house-steward, the valet, and the butler.

A 'plain' cook would earn between £20 and £40 per annum, a 'professed' cook a little more and a male chef in a large, wealthy establishment could earn up to £100. As with male servants, it was always considered far grander to have a male chef and as the fare of a household was very important for the social status of the family, good chefs were in great demand by the aristocracy and the very wealthy. It is said that Antonin Carême, (1784–1833), who was once chef to the Prince Regent, Tsar Alexander I and James Rothschild, earned £1000.00 per annum, plus perquisites, and the celebrated Alexis Soyer, (1810–1858), chef and designer of the kitchen at the Reform Club, was equally well paid. But for the most part cooks were female and their lifestyle depended greatly on the size of the house and the income of their employers.

ADVICE FOR THE COOK

Cleanliness is the most essential ingredient in the art of cooking; a dirty kitchen being a disgrace both to mistress and maid.

Be clean in your person, paying particular attention to the hands, which should always be clean. Do not go about slipshod. Provide yourself with well-fitting boots. You will find them less fatiguing in a warm kitchen than loose untidy slippers.

Provide yourself with at least a dozen good-sized serviceable cooking aprons, made with bibs. These will save your gowns, and keep you neat and clean. Have them made large enough round so as to nearly meet behind.

When you are in the midst of cooking operations, dress suitably. In the kitchen, for instance, the modern crinoline is absurd, dangerous, out of place, and extravagant. It is extravagant, because the dress is, through being nearer the fire, very liable to get scorched, and when once scorched, soon rots, and wears into holes.

We say this in the kindest possible manner; for we do not object to servants wearing a moderate amount of crinoline, or following their fancies in fashion, at proper times and in proper places. We are sure cooks would study their own pockets and convenience, and obtain the good will and approbation of their mistresses, by abolishing the use of senseless encumbrances in their kitchens. It is to be hoped that the fashion set by the aristocracy of wearing no crinoline will find its way into the kitchen.

Never waste or throw away anything that can be turned to

[*127*]

account. In warm weather, any gravies or soups that are left over from the preceding day should be just boiled up, and poured into clean pans. This is particularly necessary where vegetables have been added to the preparation, as it then so soon turns sour. In cooler weather, every other day will be often enough to warm up these things.

Every morning visit your larder, change dishes and plates when necessary, empty and wipe out the bread-pan, and have all in neatness by the time your mistress comes down to order the dinner. Twice a week the larder should be scrubbed out.

If you have a spare kitchen cupboard, keep your baked pastry in it; it preserves it crisp, and prevents it from becoming wet and heavy, which it is liable to do in the larder.

In cooking, clear as you go; that is to say, do not allow a host of basins, plates, spoons, and other utensils, to accumulate on the dresser and tables whilst you are engaged in preparing the dinner. By a little management and forethought, much confusion may be saved in this way. It is as easy to put a thing in its place when it is done with, as it is to keep continually moving it to find room for fresh requisites. For instance, after making a pudding, the flour-tub, pasteboard, and rolling pin, should be put away, and any basins, spoon, &c., taken to the scullery, neatly packed up near the sink, to be washed when the proper time arrives. Neatness, order, and method should be always observed.

SAUCES, PICKLES AND BOTTLED FRUITS FOR TARTS AND COMPÔTES (OPPOSITE). A GOOD COOK ALWAYS KEPT A WELL-STOCKED STORE-CUPBOARD.

A LARGE TUB (LEFT) FOR STORING FLOUR.

Never let your stock of spices, salt, seasonings, herbs, &c., dwindle down so low, that some day, in the midst of preparing a

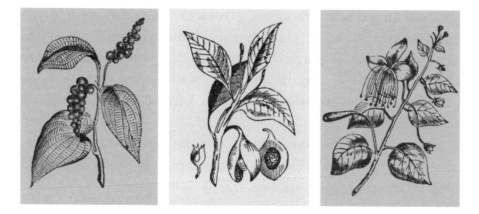

large dinner, you find yourself minus a very important ingredient, thereby causing much confusion and annoyance. Think of all you require, and acquaint your mistress in the morning, when she is with you, so that she can give out any necessary stores.

If you live in the country, have your vegetables gathered from the garden at an early hour, so that there is ample time to make your search for caterpillars &c. These disagreeable additions need never make their appearance on table in cauliflowers or cabbages, if the vegetable in its raw state is allowed to soak in salt and water for an hour or so. Of course, if the vegetables are not brought in till the last moment, this precaution cannot be taken.

Be very particular in cleansing all the vegetables free from grit. Nothing is so unpleasant, and nothing so easily avoided, if but common care be exercised.

When you have done peeling onions, wash the knife at once, and put it away to be cleaned, and do not use it for anything else until it has been cleaned. Nothing is nastier or more indicative of a slovenly and untidy cook, than to use an oniony knife in the preparation of any dish where the flavour of the onion is a disagreeable surprise.

After you have washed your saucepans, fish-kettle, &c., stand them before the fire for a few minutes, to get thoroughly dry inside,

[*130*]

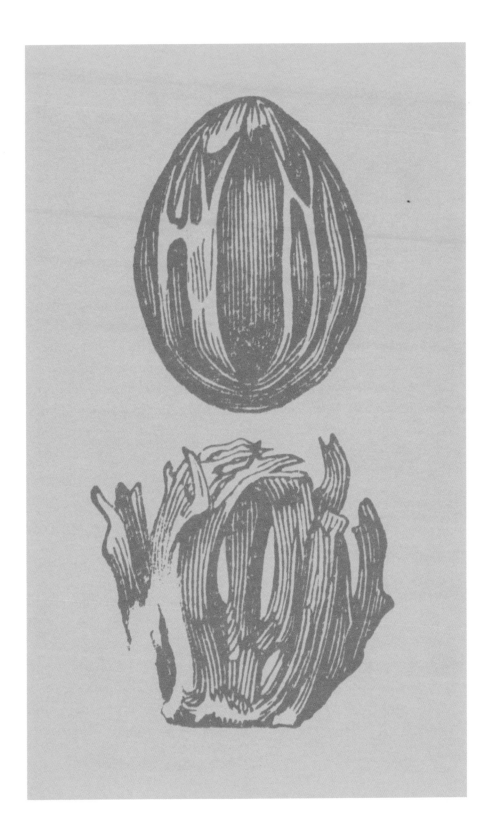

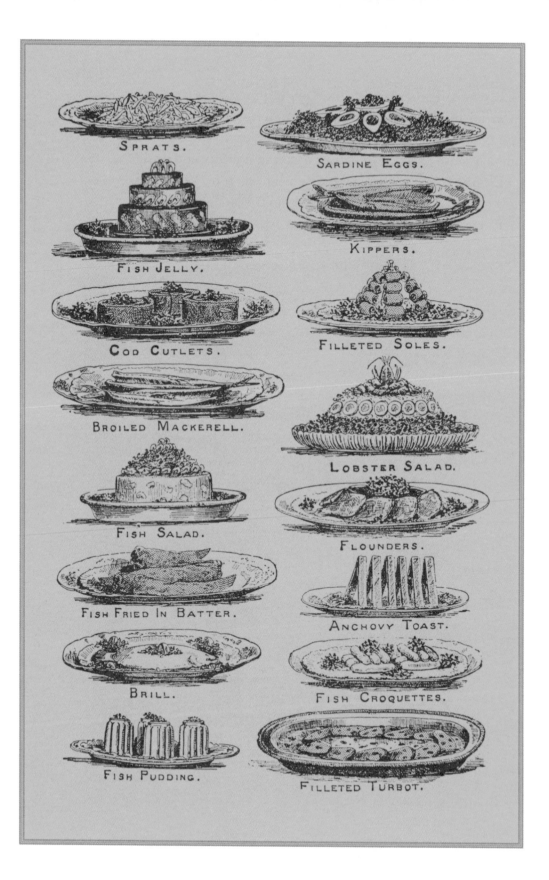

SPRATS.

SARDINE EGGS.

FISH JELLY.

KIPPERS.

COD CUTLETS.

FILLETED SOLES.

BROILED MACKERELL.

LOBSTER SALAD.

FISH SALAD.

FLOUNDERS.

FISH FRIED IN BATTER.

ANCHOVY TOAST.

BRILL.

FISH CROQUETTES.

FISH PUDDING.

FILLETED TURBOT.

before putting them away. They should then be kept in a dry place, in order that they may escape the deteriorating influence of rust, and thereby by quickly destroyed. Never leave saucepans dirty from one day's use to be cleaned the next; it is slovenly and untidy.

Empty soups or gravies into a basin as soon as they are done; never allow them to remain all night in the stock-pot.

In copper utensils. If the tin has worn off, have it immediately replaced.

Pudding-cloths and jelly-bags should have your immediate attention after being used; the former should be well washed, scalded and hung up to dry. Let them be perfectly aired before being folded up and put in the drawer, or they will have a disagreeable smell when next wanted. No soda should be used in washing pudding-cloths.

After washing up your dishes, wash your dish-tubs with a little soap and water and soda, and scrub them often. Wring the dish-cloth, after this also, and wipe the tubs out. Stand them up to dry after this operation. The sink-brush and sink must not be neglected. Do not throw anything but water down the sink, as the pipe is liable to get choked, thereby causing expense and annoyance to your mistress.

Do not be afraid of hot water in washing up dishes and dirty cooking utensils. As these are essentially greasy, lukewarm water

FISH COOKED IN
VARIOUS WAYS
(OPPOSITE) AND
BEEF DISHES
(LEFT).

[*133*]

cannot possibly have the effect of cleansing them effectually. Do not be chary also of changing and renewing the water occasionally. You will thus save yourself much time and labour in the long run.

Clean your coppers with turpentine and fine brick-dust, rubbed on with a flannel, and polish them with a leather and a little dry brick-dust.

Clean your tins with soap and whitening, rubbed on with a flannel; wipe them with a clean dry soft cloth, and polish with a dry leather and powdered whitening. Mind that neither the cloth nor leather is greasy.

Do not scrub the inside of your frying-pans, as after this operation, any preparation fried is liable to catch or burn in the pan. If the pan has become black inside, rub it with a hard crust of bread, and wash in hot water, mixed with a little soda.

Punctuality is an indispensable quality in a cook; therefore, if the kitchen be not provided with a clock, beg your mistress to purchase one. There can be no excuse for dinner being half an hour behind time.

If you have a large dinner to prepare, much must be got ready the day before, and many dishes are a great deal better for being made thus early. To soups and gravies, this remark is particularly applicable. Ask your mistress for the bill of fare the day before, and see immediately what you can commence upon.

To all these directions the Cook should pay great attention; nor should they, by any means, be neglected by the Mistress of the Household, who ought to remember that cleanliness in the kitchen gives health and happiness to home, whilst economy will immeasurably assist in preserving them.

The cook, however, is at the head of the kitchen; and in proportion to her possession of the qualities of cleanliness, neatness, order, regularity, and celerity of action, so will her influence appear in the

AN ARRAY OF
POULTRY AND
GAME DISHES,
INCLUDING SUCH
DELICACIES AS
ROAST LARK
AND SNIPE.

Pheasant.

Ptarmigan.

Partridges.

Hare Garnished.

Wild Duck.

Widgeon.

Grouse.

Snipe.

Woodcock.

Roast Turkey

Boiled Fowl.

Roast Duck

Roast Goose.

Roast Larks.

Grilled Pigeon.

Boiled Rabbit.

conduct of those who are under her; as it is upon her that the whole responsibility of the business of the kitchen rests, whilst the others must lend her both a ready and a willing assistance, and be especially tidy in their appearance, and active in their movements.

In grander establishments, 'cook' had her own room and a degree of comfort and authority. But in smaller houses she very often worked with a minimum of assistance and incorporated some of the housemaid's duties, such as cleaning and scrubbing, into her daily tasks. In some cases she would sleep in the kitchen on a truckle bed and keep her clothes and possessions in a store cupboard.

She never had the authority that was given to the housekeeper and in many instances had to ask either the housekeeper or her mistress for anything she needed from the store cupboard, as she was not allowed to hold the keys herself. This often led to the cook feeling resentful if she thought she was considered untrustworthy. She could and did supplement her earnings by selling dripping, leftover tallow and once-used tea leaves to back-door street traders, as well as what was known as 'wash' (buckets of leftovers) to the washman, who would then sell it on as pigswill or hog-wash. The latter practice was not encouraged and showed that the cook was not as frugal as she might be, as she should have used leftovers for soups and gravies.

DUTIES OF THE COOK

The quality of early rising be of the first importance to the mistress, what must it be to the servant! Let it, therefore, be taken as a long-proved truism, that without it, in every domestic, the effect of all things else, so far as work is concerned, may in a great measure be neutralized. In a cook, this quality is most essential; for an hour lost in the morning will keep her toiling, absolutely toiling, all day, to overtake that which might otherwise been achieved with ease. In

large establishments, six is a good hour to rise in the summer, and seven in the winter.

Her first duty, in large establishments and where it is requisite, should be to set her dough for the breakfast rolls, provided this has not been done on the previous night, and then to engage herself with those numerous little preliminary occupations which may not inappropriately be termed laying out her duties for the day. This

THE MISTRESS OF THE HOUSE SOMETIMES LIKED TO UNDERTAKE CERTAIN TASKS HERSELF, SUCH AS THE MAKING OF PASTRY.

will bring in the breakfast hour of eight, after which, directions must be given, and preparations made, for the different dinners of the household and family.

In those numerous households where a cook and housemaid only are kept, the general custom is, that the cook should have the charge of the dining-room. The hall, the lamps, and the doorstep are also committed to her care, and any other work there may be on the outside of the house. In the country, the summer-houses, garden-seats and chairs are also under her charge. In establishments of this kind, the cook will, after having lighted her kitchen fire, carefully brushed the range, and cleaned the hearth, proceed to prepare for breakfast.

WEIGHTS AND MEASURES

In order that the duties of the cook may be properly performed, and that he may be able to reproduce esteemed dishes with certainty, all terms of indecision should be banished from his art. Those indecisive terms expressed by a bit of this, some of that, a small piece of that, and a handful of the other, shall never be made use of, but all quantities be precisely and explicitly stated. With a desire, also, that all ignorance on this most essential part of the culinary art should disappear, and that a uniform system of weights and measures should be adopted, we give an account of the weights which answer to certain measures.

A TABLE-SPOONFUL *is frequently mentioned in a recipe, in the prescriptions by medical men, and also in medical, chemical, and gastronomical works. By it is generally meant and understood a measure or bulk equal to that which would be produced by half an ounce of water.*

A DESSERT-SPOONFUL *is half of a tablespoon; that is to say, by it is meant a measure or bulk equal to a quarter of an ounce of water.*

A TEA-SPOONFUL *is equal in quantity to a drachm of water.*

A DROP. *This is the name of a vague kind of measure, and is so called on account of the liquid being dropped from the mouth of a bottle. Its quantity, however, will vary, either from the consistency of the liquid or the size and shape of the mouth of the bottle. The College of Physicians determined the quantity of a drop to be one grain, 60 drops making one fluid drachm.*

She will thoroughly rinse the kettle, and filling it with fresh water, will put it on the fire to boil. She will then go to the breakfast-room, or parlour, and there make all things ready for the breakfast of the family. Her attention will next be directed to the hall, which she will sweep and wipe; the kitchen stairs, if there be any, will now be swept; and the hall-mats, which have been removed and shaken, will be again put in their places.

The cleaning of the kitchen, pantry, passages, and kitchen stairs must always be over before breakfast, so that it may not interfere with the other business of the day. Everything should be ready, and the whole house should wear a comfortable aspect when the heads of the house and members of the family make their appearance. Nothing, it may be depended on, will so please the mistress of an establishment as to notice that, although she has not been present to see that the work was done, attention to smaller matters has been carefully paid, with a view to giving her satisfaction and increasing her comfort. By the time that the cook has performed the duties mentioned above, and well swept and dusted her kitchen, the break-fast-bell will most likely summon her to the parlour, to "bring in" the breakfast. It is the cook's department, generally in the smaller establishments, to wait at breakfast, as the housemaid, by this time, has gone up-stairs into the bedrooms, and has there applied herself to her various duties.

But many ladies prefer the breakfast brought in by the house-maid, though cleared away and washed up by the cook. Whichever way this part of the work is managed, each servant should have her duties clearly laid down to her. The cook usually answers the bells and single knocks at the door in the early part of the morning, as the tradesmen, with whom it is her more special business to speak, call at these hours.

A LOBSTER, READY FOR THE TABLE.

It is in her preparation of the dinner that the cook begins to feel the weight and responsibility of her situation, as she must take upon herself all the dressing and the serving of the principle dishes, which her skill and ingenuity have mostly prepared. Whilst these, however, are cooking, she must be busy with her pastry, soups, gravies, ragouts &c. Stock, or what the French call consommé, being the basis of most made-dishes, must be always at hand, in conjunction with her sweet herbs and spices for seasoning. "A place for everything, and everything in its place", must be the rule, in order that time may not be wasted in looking for things when they are wanted, and in order that the whole apparatus of cooking may

A COOK MUST
ENSURE THAT
DINNER IS SERVED
PROMPTLY AND
ALL IS
SATISFACTORY TO
HER MISTRESS.

move with the regularity and precision of a well-adjusted machine—all must go simultaneously. The vegetables and sauces must be ready with the dishes they are to accompany, and in order that they may be suitable, the smallest oversight must not be made in their preparation. When the dinner-hour has arrived, it is the duty of the cook to dish-up such dishes as may, without injury, stand for some time covered on the hot plate or in the hot closet; but such as are of a more important recherché kind must be delayed until the order "to serve" is given from the drawing-room. Then comes haste; but there must be no hurry—all must work with order. The cook takes charge of the fish, soups, and poultry; and the kitchen-maid of the vegetables, sauces, and gravies. These she puts into their appropriate dishes, whilst the scullery-maid waits on and assists the cook.

Everything must be timed so as to prevent its getting cold, whilst great care should be taken that, between the first and second courses, no more time is allowed to elapse than is necessary, for fear that the company in the dining-room lose all relish for what has yet to come of the dinner. When the dinner has been served, the most important feature of the daily life of the cook is at an end. She must, however, now begin to look to the contents of her larder, taking care to keep everything sweet and clean, so that no disagreeable smells may arise from the gravies, milk, or meat that there may be there. These are the principle duties of a cook in a first-rate establishment.

In smaller establishments, the housekeeper often conducts the higher department of cooking, and the cook, with the assistance of a scullery-maid, performs some of the subordinate duties of the kitchen-maid. When circumstances render it necessary, the cook engages to perform the whole of the work of the kitchen, and, in some places, a portion of the housework as well.

Great care shou
that nothing is
or suffered to b
in the kitchen.

d be taken

hrown away,

wasted

THE KITCHEN

"THE DISTINCTION OF A KITCHEN", says Count Rumford, the celebrated philosopher and physician, who wrote so learnedly on all subjects connected with domestic economy and architecture, "must always depend so much on local circumstances, that general rules can hardly by given respecting it; the principles, however, on which this distribution ought in all cases to be made are simple and easy to be understood," and, in his estimation, these resolve themselves into symmetry of proportion in the building, and convenience to the cook. The requisites of a good kitchen, however, demand something more special than is here pointed out. It must be remembered that it is the great laboratory of every household, and that much of the "weal or woe", as far as regards bodily health, depends upon the nature of the preparations concocted within its walls.

A CHEESE PRESS, USED IN THE MAKING OF HARD CHEESES.

A good kitchen, therefore, should be erected with a view to the following particulars:– 1. Convenience of distribution in its parts, with largeness of dimension. 2. Excellence of light, height of ceiling, and good ventilation. 3. Easiness of access, without passing through the house. 4. Sufficiently remote from the principle apartments of the house, that the members, visitors, or guests of the family may not perceive the odour incident to cooking, or hear the noise of culinary operations. 5. Plenty of fuel and water, which, with the scullery, pantry, and storeroom, should be so near it as to offer the smallest possible trouble in reaching them.

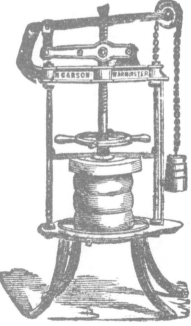

[*145*]

Victorian kitchens were situated in the basement or lower ground floor of the house. They were usually large, sparse rooms and were only used for cooking. There were other adjoining rooms, such as the scullery, or back kitchen, where messy preparations and any jobs involving water were carried out. The floors were paved with stone or brick, rubbed smooth and given one coat of oil to prevent any grease from marking it. In an ideal situation, according to J.C. Loudon, there would be skylights and the 'walls of the kitchen, for seven feet high from the ground, should not be plastered, but built of rubbed sandstone, and left bare; because plastering is continually broken in such situations, looks ill when greased, and, if whitewashed frequently, is continually scaling off in small flakes, which fall into the cooking vessels, &c.' More often than not the lower part of the walls were covered with tongue-and-groove boards painted over with a washable gloss paint or were tiled, as these surfaces were harder wearing and better for hygiene. Ceilings in the kitchens were usually very high with windows set as high as possible to draw up the excessive heat given out by the open fires and ranges, and most importantly to give good ventilation to the room.

SOME 19TH-CENTURY KITCHENS IN OTHER PARTS OF THE WORLD— AMERICA (TOP), FRANCE (BOTTOM LEFT) AND AUSTRALIA (BOTTOM RIGHT).

A MEAT SCREEN (BELOW).

A large wooden worktable was set in the middle of the room with several wooden chairs for the workers. The romantic pictures showing cook sitting in front of the fire in a comfortable, upholstered chair would have been impossible as, with all the heat, damp and smoke from the fire, such a chair would have rotted very quickly.

The cooking range was set into the fireplace, usually with a bottle-jack suspended above and a separate meat screen. On one wall there would be a large dresser holding all

the necessary implements, pots and pans and anything else needed by the cook. The shiny copper pans of the day looked impressive, but were a bane to the maids who had to clean and polish them regularly. They were lined with tin, which wore off quickly, and if not cleaned properly and re-tinned continuously, could be a serious health hazard, as they released copper acetate when cooking acidic foods.

[*148*]

When fuel and food are procured, the next consideration is, how the latter may be best preserved, with a view to its being suitably dressed. More waste is often occasioned by the want of judgement, or necessary care in this particular, than by any other causes. In the absence of proper places for keeping provisions, a hanging safe, suspended in an airy situation, is the best substitute. A well-ventilated larder, dry and shady, is better for meat and poultry, which require to be kept for some time; and the utmost skill in culinary art will not compensate for the want of proper attention to this particular. Though it is advisable that animal food should be hung up in the open air till its fibres have lost some degree of their toughness, yet, if it is kept till it loses its natural sweetness, its flavour has become deteriorated, and, as a wholesome comestible, it has lost many of its qualities conducive to health. As soon, therefore, as the slightest trace of putrescence is detected, it has reached its highest degree of

A FISH KETTLE—
AN ESSENTIAL
PIECE OF KITCHEN
EQUIPMENT FOR
THE POACHING OF
WHOLE FISH SUCH
AS SALMON.

[*149*]

tenderness, and should be dressed immediately. During the sultry summer months, it is difficult to procure meat that is not either tough or tainted. It should, therefore, be well examined when it comes in, and if flies have touched it, the part must be cut off, and the remainder well washed. In very cold weather, meat and vegetables touched by the frost, should be brought into the kitchen early in the morning, and soaked in cold water. In loins of meat, the long pipe that runs by the bone should be taken out, as it is apt to taint; as also the kernels of beef. Rumps and edge-bones of beef, when bruised, should not be purchased.

> With no reliable refrigeration and waste being considered a sin, it was very important to make sure there were facilities for all the provisions to be stored properly and nothing allowed to rot.

All these things ought to enter into consideration of every household manager; and great care should be taken that nothing is thrown away, or suffered to be wasted in the kitchen, which might, by proper management, be turned to a good account. The shank-bones

ASH'S SELF-
FEEDING CABINET
REFRIGERATOR—
AN INGENIOUS
EARLY FORM OF
REFRIGERATION
USING ICE WATER.

of mutton, so little esteemed in general, give richness to soups and gravies, if well soaked and brushed before they are added to the boiling. They are also particularly nourishing for sick persons. Roast-beef bones, or shank-bones of ham, make excellent stock for pea-soup. When the white of eggs are used for jelly, confectionery, or other purposes, a pudding or a custard should be made, that the yolks may be used.

All things likely to be wanted should be in readiness: sugars of different sorts; currants washed, picked, and perfectly dry; spices pounded, and kept in very small bottles closely corked, or in canisters, as we have already directed. Not more of these should be purchased at a time than are likely to be used in the course of a month. Much waste is always prevented by keeping every article in the place best suited to it.

Vegetables keep best on a stone floor, if the air be excluded; meat, in a cold dry place; as also salt, sugar, sweetmeats, candles, dried meats and ham. Rice, and all sorts of seeds for pudding, should be closely covered to preserve them from insects.; but even this will not preserve them from being affected by these destroyers, if they are long and carelessly kept. Pears and grapes should be strung, and hung up in a cold dry place. Apples should be laid on straw, after being carefully wiped, and should not touch each other.

GOLDEN RULES FOR THE KITCHEN

Without *cleanliness* and *punctuality* good Cooking is *impossible*.

Leave nothing *dirty; clean and clear as you go*.

A time for everything, and *everything in .ime*.

A good Cook *wastes nothing*.

An hour *lost in the morning* has to be run after *all day*.

Haste *without hurry* saves worry, fuss and flurry.

Stew *boiled* is Stew *spoiled*.

Strong fire for *Roasting; clear* fire for *Broiling*.

Wash Vegetables in *three* waters.

Boil fish *quickly*, meat *slowly*.

KITCHEN LORE
FROM
MRS BEETON.

[*151*]

Looking at the vast selection of designer kitchen gadgets on the market today, it is interesting to note that the shape of many everyday items has not changed greatly, or been improved upon, since the days of those illustrated in Mrs Beeton's Book of Household Management, printed in 1869, nearly 140 years ago. The materials they are now made from may have improved, but looking at articles such as the pestle and mortar, the colander, the grater and the omelette pan, to mention just a few, very little has changed. Even with the aid of all the modern gadgets for everything, it would be hard to surpass the extraordinary culinary skills and elaborate presentation of food that the Victorians presented at their tables.

KITCHEN UTENSILS

We commence our list with this most important kitchen utensil, as without a good set of Weights and Scales it is not possible to ensure success in cooking. Preciseness in proportioning the various ingredients, in order that no one particular flavour shall predominate should be the cook's aim. We repeat, therefore, it is absolutely necessary to have scales, even if other utensils be dispensed with. The cook should bear in mind always to put the weights away in their respective places after she has used them, and to keep her scales in thorough order. In weighing butter, lard, dripping, meat, suet, or anything that is greasy in nature, the cook should place a piece of paper in the scales before putting in the butter, lard, or other substance to be weighed. By doing this, she will save herself much labour, and will be enabled to keep the metal scale brighter.

Saucepans of various kinds rank among the most important articles in the kitchen, for very little cooking can be done without them. There are many kinds and varieties of saucepans, and we give illustrations of a few that are generally found to be the most useful.

FISH FRYER AND DRAINER.

WIRE FRYING BASKET.

WARREN'S CORRUGATED
BACHELOR'S BROILER.

WARREN'S ROUND COOKING
POT.

BOWER'S PATENT POTATO
STEAMER — A, BOILING;
B, STEAMING.

BOWER'S PATENT FISH, POUL-
TRY OR VEGETABLE STEAMER.

WARREN'S NEW BELLIED COOKING POT.

WARREN'S CURRY PAN.

PERKINS' SANITARY SEAMLESS STEEL SAUCEPAN.

WARREN'S OBLONG FISH KETTLE.

PERKINS SEAMLESS STEEL STEW-PAN.

D

DIGESTER. This utensil is a kind of stockpot, made of iron, and a lid of which fits closely into a groove at the top of the digester. No steam escapes, therefore, by the lid, and it is only through the valve at the top of the cover that the superfluous steam passes off. It is a very valuable utensil, inasmuch as by using it, a larger quantity of wholesome and nourishing food may be obtained at much cheaper rates than is possible without it.

This utensil, when in use, should not be placed over a fierce fire, as that would injure the quality of the preparation; for whatever is cooked must be done by a slow and gradual process, the liquid being just kept at the simmering point. These digesters are made in all sizes, and may be obtained to hold from 3 quarts to 10 gallons. The smaller kinds are very useful for making gravies in.

THE STOCK-POT, as its name implies, is used in the preparation of stock, which forms the foundation of soups, gravies, &c. Stock is made of meat, bones, vegetables, spices, &c., and should always be prepared the day before it is wanted. A good cook should never be without stock: therefore she should make it her first business every morning to put the stock-pot on the stove, and bear in

FROM LEFT TO
RIGHT: A PLATE
CARRIER, A
TONGUE PRESS
(FOR PREPARING
PRESSED OX
TONGUE), AND
A FREEZING
MACHINE
(FOR MAKING
ICE CREAM).

mind never to allow the preparation to remain in the vessel all night. Stock-pots are always made in iron and copper.

BOILING-POT. In large families this utensil comes into almost daily requisition. It is used for boiling large joints, hams, puddings, &c., and is made of iron.

STEW-PAN. This differs from a saucepan in having straight sides, and a flat lid with a handle. This kind of stew-pan is much in vogue, it being convenient for many purposes. One great advantage is, that the lid may at any time be lifted off without danger of burning the fingers, which, with the common saucepan, cannot sometimes be avoided. In French kitchens the lid is of bright metal, which forms a nice addition to the kitchen mantlepiece or the pot-board under the dresser.

DOUBLE SAUCEPAN. This saucepan is, on a small scale, what the bain-marie is on the large scale. The smaller saucepan fitting into the larger one is lined with enamel, which is nice for boiling custards, milk, or any preparation that is liable to easily burn or catch. When in use, the lower saucepan is half filled with water. In warming up good gravies, or any dish that wants much nicety and care, these saucepans will be found very useful.

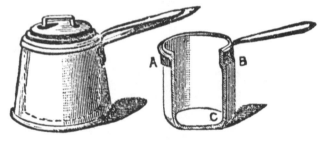

DOUBLE SAUCEPAN OR MILK PAN.

IMPROVED POTATO-STEAMER. The invention of this new potato-steamer, enabled cooks to send to table the potatoes, dry, hot, and mealy, a result which is not always obtained in the ordinary way. The arrangement is very simple, and easily understood. By drawing out a handle when the potatoes are cooked, the steam is allowed to escape from an aperture in the side, and the heat from the boiling water below converts the steamer into a dry hot closet, so completely evaporating the moisture remaining in them.

STOCK-POT.   BAIN-MARIE   STEW-PAN.

BRAIZING PAN.   BLOCK-TIN SAUCEPAN.   BOILING-POT.

DOUBLE, OR MILK, SAUCEPAN.   IRON SAUCEPAN, WITH STEAMER.

OMELETTE PAN.   PRESERVING PAN AND SPOON.

SAUTÉ-PAN.   FRICANDEAU PAN.

SALMON KETTLE.   TURBOT KETTLE.   FISH KETTLE.

THE TURBOT-KETTLE. is arranged to suit the shape of the fish from which it takes its name. It is shallow, very broad, and is fitted inside with a drainer the same as other fish-kettles. This kettle is also fitted with a drainer inside, which is pulled up when the fish is sufficiently cooked. The drainer is then laid across the kettle and the fish lifted on to the dish with the slice.

WIRE VEGETABLE-STRAINER. This is a wire frame made to fit inside a pan, in which parsley or other vegetables are fried in oil.

BOTTLE-JACK AND WHEEL. When the joint is hooked on, the jack requires winding up, which operation must be repeated once or twice during the time the meat is cooking.

MEAT SCREEN. When the meat is roasting, this screen is placed in front of the fire, to condense that heat as much as possible. It is made of wood, lined with tin, and is fitted with a shelf which acts as a warmer for the plates and dishes.

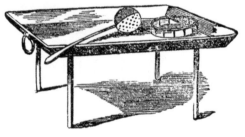

THE DRIPPING-PAN is the receptacle for the droppings of fat and gravy that fall from the roast meat. The pan is arranged with a well in the centre, covered with a lid; round this well is a series of small holes, which allow the dripping to pass into the well free from cinders or ashes. When the meat is required to be basted, the lid of the well is lifted up, the dripping is free from impurities, and the surface of the joint is moistened to prevent it from scorching. The basting-ladle is half covered over at the top with a piece of metal perforated with small holes, so that, should a small piece of cinder get into the ladle it will lodge there, and not fall on the meat.

FRYING-PANS AND OMELET-PANS. Frying-pans are made both in iron and copper, the former, perhaps, being the most generally used. Omelet-pans are very shallow, with slanting sides, convenient for turning pancakes, omelets, &c.

MORE OF THE EXTENSIVE BATTERIE DE CUISINE RECOMMENDED BY MRS BEETON (OPPOSITE), AND A DRIPPING PAN (ABOVE).

[*157*]

COPPER PRESERVING-PAN. Jam, jellies, marmalades, and preserves, are made in these utensils, which should be kept scrupulously clean, and well maintained before being used.

STEAK TONGS. To prevent the juices of the steak from being lost by pricking the meat with a fork, in turning it around on the gridiron, steak-tongs are brought into requisition for handling the steaks during the grilling process. By making use of these the gravy is kept on the meat.

SUET CHOPPER OR MINCING KNIFE. A tool like this is convenient for chopping suet, and any ingredient that requires to be finely minced. Being made with a

wooden handle, the hand does not get so fatigued as by using an ordinary knife, and the business of mincing is accomplished in a much shorter time, These utensils should be kept nice and sharp, and should be ground occasionally.

BREAD GRATER. Nicely grated bread-crumbs rank as one of the most important ingredients in any puddings, seasonings, stuffings, forcemeats &c., and add much to the appearance of nicely fried fish. For the purpose of crumbing the bread smoothly and evenly, the bread-grater is used, which is perforated on both sides with holes.

COLANDER. This useful article comes into daily requisition. It is a round tin basin with handles, perforated at the bottom and round the sides with small holes. It is used for straining vegetables, these being poured into the colander when they are cooked, and allowed to remain for a minute or two until all the water is drained from them, when they are dished.

PESTLE AND MORTAR. These are made of iron, brass, marble, and Wedgewood ware. The two latter kinds are decidedly to be preferred, as they can be so easily kept clean. This utensil is used for pounding sugar, spices, and other ingredients required in many preparations of the culinary art.

VEGETABLE CUTTER. Vegetables are cut out in fanciful shapes, by the means of these little cutters. Stewed steaks, and the such like dishes, where the vegetables form an important addition, are much improved in appearance by having them shaped.

CUCUMBER SLICE. For shredding cucumbers into the thinnest possible slices, this little machine is used. It is made of wood, with a steel knife running across the centre. After the cucumber is pared and levelled, it should be held upright, and worked backwards and forwards on the knife, bearing sufficiently hard to make an impression on the cucumber.

A STEAMER,
WHICH COULD BE
USED FOR FISH OR
VEGETABLES.

PASTEBOARD AND ROLLING-PIN. This is so familiar a piece of kitchen furniture, that very little description will be required of it. The best kinds of pasteboards are made in boxwood, and require to be very nicely kept. They should not hang in a damp place, as then they are liable to get mildewed, which will very seldom scrub out.

PASTE JAGGER. Used for trimming the cutting pastry. The little wheel at the end is made to revolve, and is used for making pastry which has to be divided after it is baked.

PEPPER MILL. This mill can be regulated to grind either fine or coarse pepper.

WIRE DISH COVER. This article belongs strictly to the larder, and is intended for covering over meat, pastry &c., to protect it from flies and dust. It is a most necessary addition to the larder, especially in summer time.

KNIFE BASKET. This is made of wicker outside, lined with tin, and is a very clean neat-looking knife basket. It is very easily washed and kept in proper order, which is not always the case with the wooden boxes.

PATTY-PANS are made of tin, and used for cheesecakes, little tarts, mince pies, &c. Some are fluted and some plain, and they are manufactured in all sizes and of different shapes, both oval and round.

COFFEE AND TEA CANISTERS. Japanned tin is the metal of which these canisters are composed. The flavour of the tea and the aroma of the coffee are much preserved by keeping them in tin canisters.

HOT-WATER DISH. In cold weather such joints as venison, a haunch, saddle, or leg of mutton, should always be served on a Hot-Water Dish, as they are so liable to chill. This dish is arranged with a double bottom, which is filled with very hot water, just before the joint is sent to table, and so keeping that and the gravy deliciously hot. Although an article of this description can hardly be ranked as a kitchen utensil, still the utility of it is so obvious, no properly furnished house should be without.

POTATO PASTRY-PAN. The preparation of meat and potatoes made in this pastry-pan is extremely savoury and delicious. The meat is placed at the bottom of the pan, with seasoning, butter, and a little water, and the perforated plate, with its valve-pipe screwed on, is laid over the meat. Some mashed potatoes, mixed with milk, are next arranged on the perforated plate, filling up the whole space to the top of the tube, and finishing the surface in an ornamental manner. If carefully baked, the potatoes will be covered with a delicate brown crust, retaining all the savoury steam arising from the meat. We may here inform our readers that either fresh or cooked meat may be dressed in the above manner; and, in the latter case, the pan will be found of great advantage, as it adds another dish to the list of "Cold Meat Cookery."

MINCING MACHINE. By a recently invented mincing machine, suet may be cut, mincemeat minced, and sausages be made at home. The machine is screwed to the table with the clamp-screw. To make sausages, the meat is cut into pieces about an inch square, some stale bread soaked and mixed with it, as also the seasoning. The skin is run on

A HOT-WATER DISH (ABOVE) AND A MINCING MACHINE (LEFT).

the nozzle, a small quantity of meat is placed in the hopper, which is kept supplied, the handle being turned to the right. The meat is thus chopped and forced into the skin. In cutting suet the nozzle is not used. Plenty of flour should be used, and the suet and flour passed at the same time through the machine. Mincemeat and other ingredients, to be cut, are also passed through the machine, the nozzle not being required.

BAIN MARIE PAN AND SAUCEPANS. The Bain Marie is not used nearly so much in England as it deserves to be. In serving a large dinner it is a most useful, and indeed, necessary article. The pan is filled with boiling water, and stands on the hot-plate of kitchener. Herein are placed the saucepans holding the sauces, gravies, entrées, &c., and the Bain Marie keeps them at a proper heat, without any risk of burning, or any of the dishes losing their flavour. If the hour of dinner is uncertain in any establishment, nothing is so sure and proper a means of preserving the flavour of all dishes as the employment of the Bain Marie. They are made in block tin, with copper pan.

FILTER. A filter may be declared to be necessary in every house. There is but little trouble in keeping it clean; and there can be, by the light of recent medical and chemical experiences, no doubt of its great utility in the preservation of health and wholesomeness.

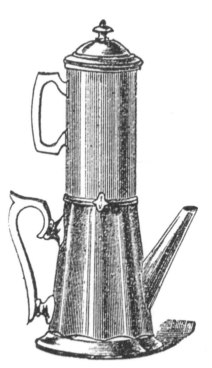

A CAFETIÈRE
STYLE OF COFFEE
MAKER.

SLACK'S CONCISE LIST OF KITCHEN REQUISITES

THE FOLLOWING LIST, supplied by Messrs. Richard & John Slack, 336, Strand, will show the articles required for the kitchen of a family in the middle class of life, although it does not contain all the things that may be deemed necessary for some families, and may contain more than are required for others. As Messrs. Slack themselves, however, publish a useful illustrated catalogue, which may be had at their establishment gratis, and which it will be found advantageous to consult by those about to furnish, it supersedes the necessity of our enlarging that which we give:—

	S.	D.
1 Tea-kettle	6	6
1 Toasting-fork	1	0
1 Bread-grater	1	0
1 Pair of Brass Candlesticks	3	6
1 Teapot and Tray	6	6
1 Bottle-jack	9	6
6 Spoons	1	6
2 Candlesticks	2	6
1 Candle-box	1	4
6 Knives and Forks	5	3
2 Sets of Skewers	1	0
1 Meat-chopper	1	9
1 Cinder-sifter	1	3
1 Coffee-pot	2	3
1 Colander	1	6
3 Block-tin Saucepans	5	9
5 Iron Saucepans	12	0
1 Ditto and Steamer	6	6
1 Large Boiling-pot	10	0
4 Iron Stewpans	8	9
1 Dripping-pan and Stand	6	6
1 Dustpan	1	0
1 Fish and Egg-slice	1	9
2 Fish-kettles	10	0
1 Flour-box	1	0
3 Flat-irons	3	6
2 Frying-pans	4	0
1 Gridiron	2	0
1 Mustard-pot	1	0
1 Salt-cellar	0	8
1 Pepper-box	0	6
1 Pair of Bellows	2	0
3 Jelly-moulds	8	0
1 Plate-basket	5	6
1 Cheese-toaster	1	10
1 Coal-shovel	2	6
1 Wood Meat-screen	30	0

THE SET £8 11s 1d

THE KITCHEN RANGE

A word as to the Kitchen Range will be in place. On this most important kitchen fixture depends much of the success or failure of the cook's performances. To those who would have a nicely-cooked dinner every day, we heartily recommend the closed stoves, commonly known as "Leamington" ranges. By making use of one of these, much trouble and labour are saved. Their advantages, indeed, are so great, that an inexperienced cook would scarcely fail to serve up a passable dinner if she had a "Leamington" at her disposal; whilst the same person, with an open range, would have acquitted herself in a wretched manner. We will briefly state the advantages these ranges possess over the open stoves, and we have not the least doubt but that our readers will agree with us in acknowledging their

A CONSTANTINE'S TREASURE RANGE, WITH ROASTER AND OVEN.

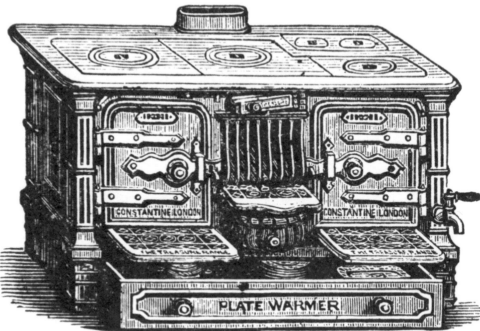

superiority, particularly for those persons who are not too well acquainted with the culinary art.

FIRST ADVANTAGE.- There is no fear of having any dish smoked sent to table. The range being made with a hot-plate all along the top, and the fire not being exposed, the possibility of having any concoction spoiled by its being smoked is quite precluded. On the other hand, when open stoves are in use, and are managed by rather unskilful hands, it is not too much to say that a smoked dish is almost as frequently the rule as the exception.

SECOND ADVANTAGE.- Many

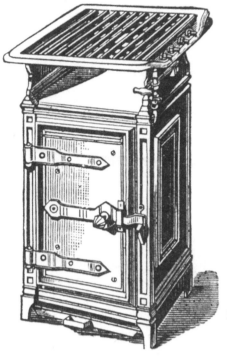

FLETCHER'S NO.4 GAS COOKING RANGE.

saucepans and vessels may be kept boiling at one time and at the proper point. Moreover, these vessels are neither soiled nor injured. On an open stove, however, the proper degree of ebullition can scarcely be sustained where there are many saucepans to attend to. Frequently the liquid is either boiling and bubbling at a galloping rate, or, is barely warm. Now the gentle simmering can be nicely kept up on any part of the "Leamington" range , when supplied with fuel for cooking a dinner. On a 4-foot range, 12 saucepans can be easily placed.

THIRD ADVANTAGE.- Saucepans, boiling pots, frying-pans, &c., last double the time when used on a hot-plate, and may be kept as clean outside as inside, there being no accumulation of soot and black. This is an immense saving of labour to the cook and of money to the mistress.

[*165*]

FOURTH ADVANTAGE.- After the cooking is done, the fire may be kept up with any cinders or small coal which could not possibly be burnt in any other range. By keeping the dampers nearly closed, a fire once made up will last for hours.

FIFTH ADVANTAGE.- Much breaking of crockery is avoided in warming plates and dishes that are to be used at dinner. There is a rack fixed above the range for this purpose, and this being quite out of the way, does not interfere with the cook when she is attending to the dinner.

A 'MISTRESS' RANGE, AS RECOMMENDED BY MRS BEETON FOR ITS RELIABILITY AND DURABILITY.

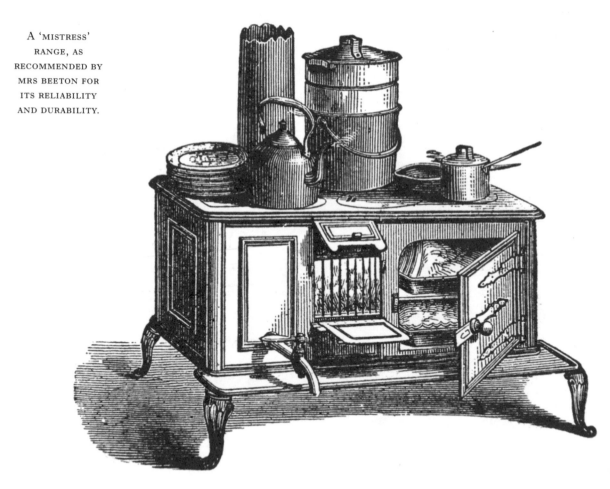

SIXTH ADVANTAGE.- The hot-plate is well calculated for an ironing stove when not in use for cooking purposes. We need scarcely say the process is delightfully clean; the irons, after being heated, merely requiring a rub with a duster. Many of our readers know what it is to iron with irons that have been heated at an open fire—what rubbing on sand-paper, in sand,&c, &c., to make the irons at all fit for use. So in this instance, again, we fairly award the palm to our favourite closed stove.

We firmly believe that English cookery will never be generally improved until all houses possess, instead of the old open range, a useful, civilized batterie de cuisine, like the "Leamington". Besides the Leamington range has a perfectly ventilated and spacious wrought-iron roaster, with moveable shelves, draw-out stand, double dripping-pan, and meat-stand. The roaster can be converted into an oven by closing the valves, when bread and pastry can be baked in it in a superior manner. It also has a large iron boiler, with brass tap and steam-pipe, round and square gridirons for chops and steaks, ash-pan, open fire for roasting, and a set of ornamental coverings, with plate-warmer attached.

In smaller houses where there were no separate servant's quarters or spare bedrooms, the cook and scullery maid would often find themselves sleeping in the kitchen, which was probably as comfortable, and certainly warmer than the rooms up in the cold attics.

Close by the kitchen would be the back staircase used by the servants to reach the upper floors and especially to carry up the food for the nursery, which could be three or four floors above the kitchen. There was always a green baize-covered door to separate the servants' quarters from the main house and no servant ever used the main staircase unless going about their household duties.

'Cleanliness is
saith the prove
in the next deg

ext to godliness'

o, and 'order' is

ce...

HOUSEMAIDS

ON LEISURE DAYS, the housemaid should be able to do some needle-work for her mistress,—such as turning and mending sheets and darning the house-linen, or assist her in anything she may think fit to give her to do. For this reason it is almost essential that a housemaid, in a small family, should be an expert needle-woman; as, if she be a good manager and an active girl, she will have time on her hands to get through plenty of work.

The more servants a household could boast of, the more prestige and standing it gave the family in society. It was always considered desirable to have at least one male servant, and as the family climbed up the social ladder so the number of servants increased. No one household was exactly the same and in some aristocratic establishments there could be up to thirty indoor staff, including a chamber maid, a parlour maid, upper and lower housemaids and a between maid, known as a 'tweeny'. There would be kitchen maids, a scullery maid, laundry maids, a maid-of-all-work, several nurse maids and a lady's maid.

However many names there were for maids, and descriptions of their specific duties, the house, no matter how large or small, had to be maintained to very high standards if the family were to be accepted in 'polite society'.

DIVIDING THE WORK

Housemaids, in large establishments, have usually one or more assistants; in this case they are upper and lower housemaids. Dividing the work between them, the upper housemaid will probably reserve for herself the task of dusting the ornaments and cleaning the furniture of the principal apartments; but it is her duty to see that every department is properly attended to. The number of assistants depends on the number in the family, as well as on the style in which the establishment is kept up. In wealthy families it is not unusual for every grown-up daughter to have her waiting-maid, whose duty it is to keep her mistress's apartments in order, thus abridging the housemaid's duties. In others, perhaps, one waiting-maid attends on two or three, when the housemaid's assistance will be more requisite. In fact, every establishment has some customs peculiar to itself; the general duties are the same in all, perfect cleanliness and order being the object.

It will be necessary for the housemaid to divide her work, so that she may not have too much to do on certain days, and not sufficient to fill up her time on other days, and to be methodical and regular in her work, the housemaid should have certain days for doing certain rooms thoroughly, For instance, the drawing-room on Monday; two bedrooms on Tuesday, two on Wednesday, and so on, reserving a day for thoroughly cleaning the plate, bedroom candlesticks, &c., &c., which she will have to do where there is no parlour-maid or footman kept. By this means the work will be divided, and there will be no unnecessary bustling and hurrying; as is the case where the work is done any time, without rule or regulation.

If there was only one housemaid employed, she would be expected to perform all the household duties usually shared out among several other maids. She would be lucky to earn £16.00 a year, with an hour allowed for Church on Sundays and maybe one day a month holiday.

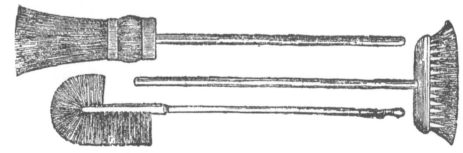

The housemaid's
brushes and
brooms.

A HOUSEMAID IN A
LATE VICTORIAN
HOUSEHOLD
TENDING THE
LAMPS ON THE
DINING TABLE.

"Cleanliness is next to godliness" saith the proverb, and "order" is in the next degree; the housemaid, then, may be said to be the hand-maiden to two of the most prominent virtues. Her duties are very numerous, and many of the comforts of the family depend on their performances: but they are simple and easy to a person naturally clean and orderly, and desirous of giving satisfaction. In all families, whatever the habits of the master and mistress, servants will find it advantageous to rise early; their daily work will thus come easy to them. If they rise late, there is a struggle to overtake it, which throws an air of haste and hurry over the whole establishment. The house-maid who studies her own ease will certainly be at her work by six o'clock in the summer, and, probably, by half-past six or seven in the winter months, having spent a reasonable time in her own chamber in dressing. Earlier than this would, probably, be an unnecessary waste of coals and candle in winter.

The first duty of the housemaid in winter is to open the shutters of all the lower rooms in the house, and take up the hearth-rugs of those rooms which she is going to "do" before breakfast. In some families, where there are only a cook and housemaid kept, and where the drawing-rooms are large, the cook has the care of the dining-room, and the housemaid that of the breakfast room, library, and draw-ing room. After the shutters are all opened, she sweeps the breakfast-room, sweeping the dust towards the fire-place, of course previ-

ously removing the fender. She should then lay a cloth (generally made of coarse wrapping) over the carpet in front of the stove, and on this should place her housemaid's box, containing black-lead brushes, leathers, emery-paper, cloth, black-lead, and all utensils necessary for cleaning a grate, with a cinder-pail on the other side.

She now sweeps up the ashes, and deposits them in her cinder-pail, which is a japanned tin pail, with a wire sifter inside, and a closely fitting-top. In this pail the cinders are sifted, and reserved for use in the kitchen or under the copper, the ashes only being thrown away. The cinders disposed of, she proceeds to black-lead the grate, producing the black lead, the soft brush for laying it on, her blacking and polishing brushes, from the box which contains her tools. The housemaid's box should be kept well stocked. Having blackened, brushed, and polished every part, and made all clean and bright, she now proceeds to lay the fire. Sometimes it is difficult to get a proper polish to black grates, particularly if they have been neglected, and allowed to rust at all.

Bright grates require unceasing attention to keep them in perfect order. A day should never pass without the housemaid rubbing with a dry leather the polished parts of a grate, as also the fender and fire-irons. A careful and atten-

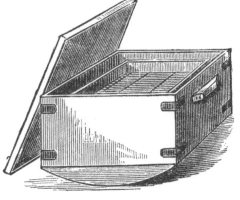

THE HOUSEMAID'S BOX (ABOVE) CONTAINED EQUIPMENT FOR CLEANING GRATES.

A CINDER PAIL (LEFT) WITH A LOOSE TRAY FOR COLLECTING ASH.

[*175*]

A HOUSEMAID ON
HER KNEES CLEAN-
ING THE GRATE—
A TASK REQUIRING
MUCH ELBOW
GREASE AS WELL
AS GRATE POLISH.

tive housemaid should have no occasion ever to use emery-paper for any part but the bars, which, of course, become blackened by the fire. (Some mistresses, to save labour, have a double set of bars, one set bright for the summer, and another black set to use when fires are in requisition.)

When bright grates are once neglected, small rust-spots begin to show themselves, which a plain leather will not remove; the following method of cleaning them must then be resorted to:- First, thoroughly clean with emery-paper; then take a large smooth pebble from the road, sufficiently large to hold in the hand, with which to rub the steel backwards and forwards one way, until the desired polish is obtained. It may appear at first to scratch, but continue rubbing, and the result will be success.

Many housemaids entered service at a very young age and knew no other life. They were grateful to have a secure job, food to eat and a roof over their head when many other young girls were starving and homeless.

If the house included a servants' hall, the lower staff were not allowed to speak during meals in the presence of their superiors. They had always to be punctual to meals and were not permitted to receive any relations, visitors or friends in the house, or in the servants'

STOVE AND STEEL POLISH

The following is also an excellent polish for bright stoves and steel articles:—

INGREDIENTS -
1 *tablespoonful of turpentine,*
1 *ditto of sweet oil,*
emery powder.

MODE.—Mix the turpentine and sweet oil together, stirring in sufficient emery powder to make the mixture of the thickness of cream. Put it on the article with a piece of soft flannel, rub off quickly with another piece, then polish with a little dry emery powder and clean leather.

hall, without the consent of the housekeeper or the butler. Followers were forbidden and if any female staff were caught fraternizing with callers, they would be immediately dismissed from service. The cost of any damages or breakages in the course of their duties was deducted from their wages.

MORNING TASKS

Fire-lighting, however simple, is an operation requiring some skill; a fire is readily made by laying a few cinders at the bottom in open order; over this a few pieces of paper, and over that again eight or ten pieces of dry wood, a course of moderate-sized pieces of coal, taking care to leave hollow spaces between for air at the centre; and taking care to lay the whole well back in the grate, so that the smoke may go up the chimney, and not into the room. This done, fire the paper with a match from below, and, if properly laid, it will soon burn up; the stream of flame from the wood and paper soon communicating to the coals and cinders, provided there is plenty of air at the centre.

A new method of lighting a fire is sometimes practised with advantage, the fire lighting from

A HOUSEMAID HAD A LOT OF HEAVY WORK, INCLUDING BRINGING SCUTTLES OF COAL TO EACH ROOM (RIGHT) AND POLISHING FLOORS (OPPOSITE).

the top and burning down, in place of being lighted and burning up from below. This is arranged by laying the coals at the bottom, mixed with a few good-sized cinders, and the wood at the top, with another layer of coals and some paper over it; the paper is lighted in the usual way, and soon burns down to a good fire, with some economy of fuel, as is said.

The several fires lighted, the housemaid proceeds with her dusting, and polishing the several pieces of furniture in the breakfast-parlour, leaving no corner unvisited. Before sweeping the carpet, it is good practice to sprinkle it all over with tea-leaves, which not only lay all dust, but give a slightly fragrant smell to the room. It is now in order for the reception of the family, and where there is neither footman or parlour-maid, she now proceeds to the dressing-room, and lights her mistress's fire, if she is in the habit of having one to dress by. Her mistress is called, hot water placed in the dressing-room for her use, her clothes—as far as they are under the housemaid's charge—put before the fire, hanging a fire-guard on the bars where there is one, while she proceeds to prepare the breakfast.

In summer the housemaid's work is considerably abridged; she throws open the windows of the several rooms not occupied as bedrooms, that they may receive the fresh morning air before they are occupied; she prepares the breakfast-room by sweeping the carpet, rubbing tables and chairs, dusting mantel-shelf and picture frames with a light brush, dusting the furniture and sweeping the

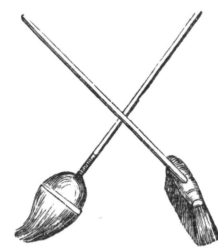

DUSTING AND SWEEPING ALL THE ROOMS WAS A DAILY TASK (OPPOSITE). AMONG THE HOUSEMAID'S EQUIPMENT WERE CARPET BROOMS (LEFT) AND A BANNISTER BRUSH (ABOVE).

ANOTHER OF THE
HOUSEMAID'S
RESPONSIBILITIES
WAS KEEPING THE
FRONT STEPS OF
THE HOUSE CLEAN.

rug; she cleans the grate when necessary, and replaces the white
paper or arranges the shavings with which it is filled, leaving everything clean and tidy for breakfast.

After the breakfast-room is finished, the housemaid should proceed to sweep down the stairs, commencing at the top, whilst the
cook has the charge of the hall, door-step and passages. After this
she should go into the drawing-room, cover up every article of furniture that is likely to spoil, with large dusting sheets, and put the

chairs together, by turning them seat to seat, and, in fact, make as much room as possible, by placing all the loose furniture in the middle of the room, whilst she sweeps the corners and sides. When this is accomplished, the furniture can then be put back in its place, and the middle of the room swept, sweeping the dirt, as before said, towards the fireplace. The same rules should be observed in cleaning the drawing-room grates as we have just stated; putting down the cloth, before commencing, to prevent the carpet from getting soiled.

In the country, a room would not require sweeping thoroughly like this more than twice a week; but the housemaid should go over it every morning with a dust-pan and broom, taking up every crumb and piece she may see.

After the sweeping she should leave the room, shut the door, and proceed to lay the breakfast.

BREAKFAST

When there is neither footman not parlour-maid kept the duty of laying the breakfast cloth rests on the housemaid. Before laying the cloth for breakfast, the heater of the tea-urn is to be placed in the hottest part of the kitchen fire; or, where the kettle is used, boiled on the kitchen fire, and then removed to the parlour, where it is kept hot. Having washed herself free from the dust arising from the morning's work, the housemaid collects the breakfast things on her tray, takes the breakfast cloth from the napkin-press, and carries them all on the tray into the parlour; arranges them on the table, placing a sufficiency of knives, forks, and salt-cellars for

A KETTLE FOR THE KITCHEN RANGE.

[*183*]

the family, and takes the tray back to the pantry; gets a supply of milk, cream, and bread; fills the butter-dish, taking care that the salt is plentiful, and soft and dry, and that hot plates and egg-cups are ready where warm meat or eggs are served, and that butter-knife and bread-knife are in their places on the table.

A HOT-WATER
URN FOR THE
BREAKFAST TABLE
WHICH THE
HOUSEMAID HAD
TO FILL.

And now the housemaid should give the signal for breakfast, holding herself ready to fill the urn with hot water, or hand the kettle, and take in the rolls, toast, and other eatables, with which the cook supplies her, when the breakfast-room bell rings; bearing in mind that she is never to enter the parlour with dirty hands or with a dirty apron, and that everything is to be handed on a tray; that she has to hand everything she may be required to supply, on the left hand of the person she is serving, and that all is done quietly and without bustle or hurry. In some families, where there is a large number to attend on, the cook waits at breakfast whilst the housemaid is busy upstairs in the bedrooms, or sweeping, dusting, and putting the drawing-room in order.

There were strict guidelines in the hierarchy of the servants and there was also a 'pecking order' between the servants of different houses. This was gauged by the number of staff kept per head of the family. For example, six servants per member of a family was held to be superior to four servants per head.

Breakfast served, the housemaid proceeds to the bed-chambers, throws up the sashes, if not already done, pulls up the blinds, throwing back curtains at the same time, and opens the beds, by removing the clothes, placing them over a horse, or, failing that, over the backs of chairs. She now proceeds to empty the slops. In doing this, everything is emptied into the slop-pail, leaving a little scalding-hot water for a minute in such vessels as require it; adding a drop of turpentine to the water, when that is not sufficient to cleanse them. The basin is emptied, well rinsed with clean water, and carefully wiped; the ewers emptied and washed; finally the water-jugs themselves emptied out and rinsed, and wiped dry. As soon as this is done, she should remove and empty the pails, taking care that they are well washed, scalded, and wiped as soon as they are empty. Next follows bed-making, at which the cook or kitchen-maid, where one is kept, usually assists; but, before beginning, velvet chairs, or other things injured by dust, should be removed to another room.

BUCKET FOR EMPTYING THE SLOPS FROM THE BEDROOMS EACH MORNING.

Once a week, when a bedroom is to be thoroughly cleaned, the house-maid should commence by brushing the mattresses of the bed before it is made; she should then make it, shake the curtains, lay them smoothly on the bed, and pin or tuck up the bottom valance, so that she may be able to sweep under the bed. She should then unloop the window-curtains, shake them, and pin them high

up out of the way. After clearing the dressing-table, and the room altogether of little articles of china, &c. &c., she should shake the toilet-covers, fold them up, and lay them on the bed, over which a large dusting-sheet should be thrown. She should then sweep the room; first of all sprinkling the carpet with well-squeezed tea-leaves, or a little freshly-pulled grass, when this is obtainable. After the carpet is swept, and the grate cleaned, she should wash with soap and water, with a little soda in it, the washing-table apparatus, removing all marks or fur round the jugs, caused by the water. The water-bottles and tumblers must also have her attention, as well as the top of the washing-stand, which should be cleaned with soap and flannel if it be marble: if of polished mahogany, no soap must be used.

When these are all clean and arranged in their places, the housemaid should scrub the floor where it is not covered with carpet, under the beds, and round the wainscot. She should use as little soap and soda as possible, as too free a use of these articles is liable to give the boards a black appearance. In the country, cold soft water, a clean scrubbing-brush, and a willing arm, are all that are required to make bedroom floors look white. In winter it is not advisable to scrub rooms too often, as it is diYcult to dry them thoroughly at that season of the year, and nothing is more dangerous than to allow persons to sleep in a damp room. The housemaid should now dust the furniture, blinds, ornaments, &c.; polish the looking-glass; arrange the toilet-cover and muslin; remove the cover from the bed, and straighten and arrange the curtains and counter-pane. A bedroom should be cleaned like this every week. There are times, however, when it is necessary to have the carpet up; this should be done once a year in the country, and twice a year in large cities. The best time for these arrangements is spring and autumn.

The chambers are finished, the chamber candlesticks brought down and cleaned, the parlour lamps trimmed; – and here the housemaid's utmost care is required. In cleaning candlesticks, as in every other cleaning, she should have cloths and brushes kept for that purpose alone; the knife used to scrape them should be applied to no other purpose; the tallow-grease should be thrown into a box kept for the purpose; the same with everything connected with the lamp-trimming; the best mode of doing which she will do well to learn from the tradesman who supplies the oil; always bearing in mind, however, that without perfect cleanliness, which involves occasional scalding, no lamp can be kept in order. After scalding a lamp, it should be rinsed out with a little spirits; this will prevent the oil sputtering on first being lighted after the scalding.

The drawing-room and dining-room, inasmuch as everything there is more costly and valuable, require even more care. When the carpets are of the kind known as velvet-pile, they require to be swept firmly by a hard whisk brush, made of coconut fibre. The furniture must be carefully gone over in every corner with a soft cloth, that it may be left perfectly free from dust; or where that is beyond reach, with a brush made of long feathers, or a goose's wing. The sofas are swept in the same manner, slightly beaten, the cushions shaken and smoothed, the picture-frames swept, and everything arranged in its proper place. This of course applies to dining as well as drawing-room and morning-room. And now the housemaid may dress herself for the day, and prepare for the family dinner, at which she must attend.

[*187*]

Servants were expected to show deference to their employers at all times. They were never to speak unless spoken to, not even to say 'good morning' or good night' and were to be 'seen but not heard'. In many cases they were not even supposed to be seen and it was suggested that on encountering one of their betters, in the house or on the stairs, they should avert their eyes and turn to the wall.

This was carried to the extreme by William Beckford of Fonthill Abbey (1760–1844), reportedly the wealthiest man in England at the time. He had recesses built in his house, especially in the corridors and on the staircases, where the servants were expected to hide, so he would not see them as he passed by.

He carried this regime even into his very large garden, where 'the old tartar' insisted the gardeners carried out their duties by torchlight after dark, so he could not see them at work.

WAITING AT TABLE

We need not repeat the long instructions already given for laying the dinner-table. At the family dinner, even where no footman waits, the routine will be the same. In most families the cloth is laid with the slips on each side, with napkins, knives, forks, spoons, and wine and finger glasses on all occasions. She should ascertain that her plate is in order, glasses free from smears, water-bottles and decanters the same, and

DESPITE THE MANY DIRTY AND DEMANDING TASKS SHE HAD TO DO, THE HOUSEMAID WAS EXPECTED TO BE CLEAN AND NEATLY DRESSED AT ALL TIMES.

everything ready on her tray, that she may be able to lay her cloth properly. Few things add more to the neat and comfortable appearance of a dinner-table than well-polished plate; indeed, the state of the plate is a certain indication of a well-managed or ill-managed household.

For waiting at table, the housemaid should be neatly and cleanly dressed, and, if possible, her dress made with close sleeves, the large open ones dipping and falling into everything on the table, and being very much in the way. She should not wear creaking boots, and should move about the room as noiselessly as possible, anticipating people's wants by handing them things without being asked for them, and altogether be as quiet as possible.

The housemaid, having announced that dinner is on the table, will hand the soup, fish, meat, or side-dishes to the different members of the family; but in families who do not spend much of the day together, they will probably prefer to be alone at dinner and breakfast; the housemaid will be required, after all are helped, if her master does not wish her to stay in the room, to go on with her work of cleaning up the pantry, and answer the bell when rung. In this case she will place a pile of plates on the table or a dumb-waiter, within reach of her master and mistress, and leave the room.

EVENING WORK

The housemaid's evening service consists in washing up the dinner things, the plate, plated articles, and glasses, restoring everything to its place; cleaning up her pantry, and putting away everything for use when next required; lastly, preparing for tea, as the time approaches, by setting the things out on a tray, getting the urn or kettle ready, with cream and other things usually partaken of at that meal.

In summer-time the windows of all the bedrooms, which have been closed during the heat of the day, should be thrown open for an hour or so after sunset, in order to air them. Before dark they should be closed, the bed-clothes turned down, and the night-clothes laid in order for use when required. During winter, where fires are required in the dressing-rooms, they should be lighted an hour before the usual time of retiring, placing a fire-guard before each fire. At the same time, the night things on the horse should be placed before it to be aired, with a tin can of hot water, if the mistress is in the habit of washing before going to bed. The housemaid will probably be required to assist her mistress to undress and put her dress in order for the morrow; in which case her duties are very much those of the lady's-maid.

And now the fire is made up for the night, the fireguard replaced, and everything in the room in order for the night, the housemaid taking care to leave the night-candle and matches together in a convenient place, should they be required. It is usual in summer to remove all highly fragrant flowers from sleeping-rooms, the impression being that their scent is injurious in a close chamber.

When other maids were employed, the housemaid would usually sleep on the top floor in a dormitory, sometimes sharing a bed with another maid. If there was no specific accommodation she would often sleep in the kitchen on her 'truckle bed' and keep her belongings in a store-cupboard.

To clean Marble.

Mix with ¼ pint of soap lees, ½ gill of turpentine, sufficient pipe-clay and bullock's gall to make the whole into rather a thick paste. Apply it to the marble with a soft brush, and after a day or two, when quite dry, rub it off with a soft rag. Apply this a second or third time till the marble is quite clean.

Another method. Take two parts of soda, one of pumice-stone, and one of finely-powdered chalk. Sift these through a fine sieve, and mix them into a paste with water. Rub this well all over the marble, and the stains will be removed; then wash it with soap-and-water, and a beautiful bright polish will be produced.

To clean Floorcloth.

After having washed the floorcloth in the usual manner with a damp flannel, wet it all over with milk and rub it well with a dry cloth, when a most beautiful polish will be brought out. Some persons use for rubbing a well-waxed flannel; but this in general produces an unpleasant slipperiness, which is not the case with the milk.

To clean Decanters.

Roll up in small pieces some soft brown or blotting paper; wet them, and soap them well. Put them into the decanters about one quarter full of warm water; shake them well for a few minutes, then rinse with clear cold water; wipe the outsides with a nice dry cloth, put the decanters to drain, and when dry they will be almost as bright as new ones.

To brighten Gilt Frames.

Take sufficient flour of sulphur to give a golden tinge to about 1½ pint of water, and in this boil 4 or 5 bruised onions, or garlic, which will answer the same purpose. Strain off the liquid, and with it, when cold, wash, with a soft brush, any gilding which requires restoring, and when dry it will come out as bright as new work.

To preserve bright Grates or Fire-irons from Rust.

Make a strong paste of fresh lime and water, and with a fine brush smear it as thickly as possible over all the polished surface requiring preservation. By this simple means, all the grates and fire-irons in an empty house may be kept for months free from harm, without further care or attention.

German Furniture–Gloss.

Ingredients – ½ lb. yellow wax, 1 oz. black rosin, 2 oz. of oil of turpentine.

Mode.—Cut the wax into small pieces, and melt it in a pipkin, with the rosin pounded very fine. Stir in gradually, while these two ingredients are quite warm, the oil of turpentine. Keep this composition well covered for use in a tin or earthen pot. A little of this gloss should be spread on a piece of coarse woollen cloth, and the furniture well rubbed with it; afterwards it should be polished with a fine cloth.

Let washing-w

excuse for havi

in a muddle.

k be not an

everything

THE LAUNDRY

IF THE WASHING, or even a portion of it, is done at home, it
will be impossible for the maid-of-all-work to do her household
duties thoroughly, during the time it is about, unless she have
some assistance. Usually, if all the washing is done at home, the
mistress hires someone to assist at the wash-tub, and sees to little
matters herself, in the way of folding, starching, and ironing the fine
things. With a little management much can be accomplished, providing the mistress be industrious, energetic, and willing to lend a
helping hand. Let washing-week be not an excuse for having everything in a muddle; and although "things" cannot be cleaned so thoroughly, and so much time spent upon them, as ordinarily, yet the
house may be kept tidy and clear from litter without a great deal of
exertion either on the part of the mistress or servant.

The authoress of "Home Truths for Home Peace" says, with
respect to the great wash—"Amongst all the occasions in which it is
most difficult and glorious to keep muddle out of a family, the 'great
wash' stands pre-eminent; and as very little money is now saved by
having *everything* done at home, many ladies, with the option of
taking another servant or putting out the chief part of the washing,
have thankfully adopted the latter course."

She goes on to say, "When a gentleman who dines at home can't
bear washing in the house, but gladly pays for its being done elsewhere, the lady should gratefully submit to his wishes, and put out
anything in her whole establishment rather than put out a good and
generous husband."

Personal appearances were of utmost importance to the upper and
middle-class Victorians. At a glance one was immediately recognised
as belonging to a certain social status, so care and maintenance of
clothes required a very competent person in charge of the laundry.

THE LAUNDRY-MAID

The laundry-maid is charged with the duty of washing and getting-up the family linen, a situation of great importance where the washing is all done at home; but in large towns, where there is little convenience for bleaching and drying, it is chiefly done by professional laundresses and companies, who apply mechanical and chemical processes to the purpose. These processes, however, are supposed to injure the fabric of the linen; and in many families the fine linen, cottons, and muslins, are washed and got-up at home, even where the bulk of the washing is given out. In country and suburban houses, where greater conveniences exist, washing at home is more common,—in country places universal.

> In larger establishments there was usually a separate 'washing- house' and several full-time laundry-maids. The laundry staff often ate and slept in the laundry, under the eye of the head laundress. In smaller houses, where there was only a maid-of-all-work, she had to somehow fit this job into her already overloaded daily routine. She often slept in the laundry, scullery or kitchen, exhausted after working up to sixteen hours a day and was lucky to earn £13.00 a year

THE LAUNDRY HOUSE

The laundry establishment consists of a washing-house, an ironing and drying-room, and sometimes a drying-closet heated by furnaces. The washing-house will probably be attached to the kitchen; but it is better that it should be completely detached from it, and of one storey, with a funnel or shaft to carry off the steam. It will be of a size proportioned to the extent of the washing to be done. A range of tubs, either round or oblong, opposite, and sloping towards, the

A 19TH-CENTURY
ADVERTISEMENT
FOR 'SUNLIGHT
SOAP'.

A CHEERFUL OLD SOUL

WHOSE TASK IS LIGHTENED BY "SUNLIGHT SOAP."

IT is possible for a woman with increasing years to continue to do laundry work. Thousands who would have been laid aside under the old system of washing have proved what Sunlight Soap can do in reducing labour. The cleansing properties of Sunlight Soap save years of arduous toil. Reader, prove Sunlight Soap for yourself: by giving the best article a trial you will do yourself a real service

BEWARE!! Do not allow other Soaps, said to be the same as the "Sunlight" Soap, to be palmed off upon you. If you do, you must expect to be disappointed. See that you get what you ask for, and that the word "Sunlight" is stamped upon every tablet and printed upon every wrapper.

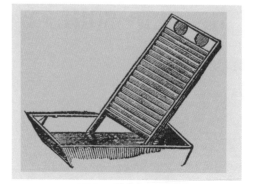

light, narrower at the bottom than the top, for convenience in stooping over, and fixed at a height suited to the convenience of the women using them; each tub having a tap for hot and cold water, and another in the bottom, communicating with the drains, for drawing off foul water. A boiler and furnace, proportioned in size to the wants of the family, should also be fixed. The flooring should be York stone, laid on brick piers, with good drainage, or asphalte, sloping gently towards a gutter connected with the drain.

Adjoining the bleaching-house, a second room, about the same size, is required for ironing, drying, and mangling. The contents of this room should comprise an ironing-board, opposite to the light; a

LAUNDRY ROOM
EQUIPMENT: A
WASHING TUB AND
BOARD (ABOVE)
AND A MANGLING
MACHINE (RIGHT).

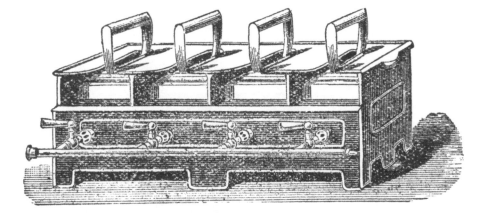

strong white deal table, about twelve or fourteen feet long, and about three and a half feet broad, with drawers for ironing-blankets; a mangle in one corner, and clothes-horses for drying and airing; cupboards for holding the various irons, starch and other articles used in ironing; a hot-plate built in the chimney, with furnace beneath it for heating the irons; sometimes arranged with a flue for carrying the hot air round the room for drying. Where this the case, however, there should be a funnel in the ceiling for ventilation and carrying off the steam, but a better arrangement is to have a hot-air closet adjoining, heated by hot-air pipes, and lined with iron, with proper arrangements for carrying off the steam, and clothes-horses on castors running in grooves, to run into it for drying purposes. This leaves the laundry free from unwholesome vapour.

AN IRON HEATER (ABOVE) AND A WRINGING MACHINE (LEFT).

[*199*]

WASHING DUTIES

The laundry-maid should commence her labours on Monday morning by a careful examination of the articles committed to her care, and enter them in the washing-book; separating the white linen and collars, sheets and body-linen into one heap, fine muslins into another, coloured cotton and linen fabrics into a third, woollens into a fourth, and the coarser kitchen and other greasy cloths into a fifth. Every article should be examined for ink or grease-spots, or for fruit or wine-stains.

Ink stains are removed by dipping the part into hot water, and then spreading it smoothly on the hand or on the back of a spoon, pouring a few drops of oxalic acid or salts of sorrel over the ink-spot, rubbing and rinsing it in cold water till removed; grease spots, by rubbing over with yellow soap, and rinsing in hot water; fruit and wine spots, by dipping in a solution of sal ammonia or spirits of wine, and rinsing.

Every article having been examined and assorted, the sheets and fine linen should be placed in one of the tubs and just covered with lukewarm water, in which a little soda has been dissolved and mixed, and left there to soak till the morning. The greasy cloths and dirtier things should be laid to soak in another tub, in a liquor composed of ½ lb of unslaked lime to every 6 quarts of water which has been boiled for two hours, then left to settle, and strained off when clear. Each article should be rinsed in the liquor to wet it thoroughly, and left to soak till the morning, just covered by it when the things are pressed together. Coppers and boilers should now be filled, and the fires laid ready to light.

Early on the following morning the fires should be lighted and as soon as hot water can be procured, washing commenced; the sheets and body-linen being wanted to whiten in the morning, should be taken first; each article being removed in succession from the lye in which it has been soaking, rinsed, rubbed, and wrung, and laid aside until the tub is empty, when the foul water is drawn off. The tub should be again filled with luke-warm water, about 80°, in which the

A LAUNDRY-MAID
BEATING THE DIRT
OUT OF THE
WASHING.

[*201*]

AN EARLY TYPE
OF WASHING
MACHINE.

articles should again be plunged, and each gone over carefully with soap, and rubbed. Novices in the art sometimes rub the linen against the skin; more experienced washerwomen rub one linen surface against the other, which saves their hands, and enables them to continue their labour much longer. Besides economizing time, two parts being thus cleaned at once.

After the first wash, the linen should be put into a second water, as hot as the hand can bear it, and again rubbed over in every part, examining every part for spots not yet removed, which require to be again soaped over and rubbed till thoroughly clean; then rinsed and wrung, the larger and stronger articles by two of the women; the smaller and more delicate articles requiring gentler treatment.

In order to remove every particle of soap, and produce a good colour, they should now be placed, and boiled for about an hour and a half, in the copper, in which soda, in the proportion of a teaspoon to every two gallons of water has been dissolved. Some very careful laundresses put the linen into a canvas bag to protect it from the scum and sides of the copper. When taken out it should again be rinsed, first in clean hot water, and then in abundance of cold water, slightly tinged with fig-blue, and again wrung dry. It should now be removed from the washing-house and hung up to dry or spread out to bleach, if there are conveniences for it; and the earlier in the day this is done, the clearer and whiter will be the linen.

Coloured muslins, cottons, and linens, require a milder treatment; any application of soda will discharge the colour, and soaking all night, even in pure water, deteriorates the more delicate tints. When ready for washing, if not too dirty, they should be put into cold water and washed very speedily, using the common yellow soap, which should be rinsed off immediately. One article should be washed at a time, and rinsed out immediately before any others are wetted. When washed thoroughly, they should be rinsed in succession, in soft water, in which common salt has been dissolved, in the proportion of a handful to three or four gallons, and afterwards wrung gently, as soon as rinsed, with as little twisting as possible, and then hung out to dry. Delicate-coloured articles should not be exposed to the sun, but dried in the shade, using clean lines and wooden pegs.

WOOL AND SILK

Woollen articles are liable to shrink, unless the flannel has been well shrunk before making up. This liability is increased where very hot water is used; cold water would thus be the best to wash woollens in; but as this would not remove the dirt, lukewarm water, about 85°, and yellow soap, are recommended.

A LAUNDRY-MAID
OPERATING
A WASHING
MACHINE.

When thoroughly washed in this, they require a good deal of rinsing in cold water, to remove the soap.

Greasy cloths, which have soaked all night in the liquid described, should now be washed out with soap-and-water as hot as the hands can bear, first in one water, and rinsed out in a second; and afterwards boiled for two hours in water in which a little soda is dissolved. When taken out, they should be rinsed in cold water, and laid out or hung up to dry.

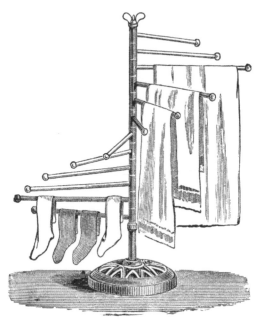

Silk handkerchiefs require to be washed alone. When they contain snuff, they should be soaked by themselves in lukewarm water two or three hours; they should be rinsed out and put to soak with the others in cold water for an hour or two; then washed in lukewarm water, being soaped as they are washed. If this does not remove all stains, they should be washed a second time in similar water, and when finished, rinsed in soft water in which a handful of common salt has been dissolved.

In washing stuff or woollen dresses, the band at the waist and the lining at the bottom should be removed, and wherever it is gathered into folds; and, in furniture, the hems and gatherings. A black silk dress, if very dirty, must be washed; but, if only soiled, soaking for four-and-twenty hours will do; if old and rusty, a pint of common spirits should be mixed with each gallon of water, which is an improvement under any circumstances. Whether soaked or washed, it should be hung up to dry, and dried without wringing. Silks and silk ribbons, both white and coloured, may be cleaned in the same manner.

Silks, when washed, should be dried in the shade, on a linen-horse, taking care that they are kept smooth and unwrinkled. If black or blue, they will be improved if laid again on the table, when dry, and sponged with gin, or whisky, or other white spirit.

The operations should be concluded by rinsing the tubs, cleaning the coppers, scrubbing the floors of the washing house, and restoring everything to order and cleanliness.

Thursday and Friday, in a laundry in full employ, are usually devoted to mangling, starching and ironing. Linen, cotton, and other fabrics, after being washed and dried, are made smooth and glossy by mangling and by ironing. The mangling process which is simply passing them between rollers subjected to a very considerable pressure, produced by weight, is confined to sheets, towels, table-linen and similar articles, which are without folds or plaits.

STARCHING

STARCHING is a process by which stiffness is communicated to certain parts of linen, as the collar and fronts of shirts, by dipping them in a paste made of starch boiled in water, mixed with a little gum Arabic, where extra stiffness is required.

When the "things to be starched" are washed, dried, and taken off the lines, they should be dipped into the hot starch squeezed out of it, and then just dipped into cold water, and immediately squeezed dry. If fine things be wrung, or roughly used, they are very liable to tear; so too much care cannot be exercised in this respect. If the article is lace, clap it between the hands a few times, which will assist to clear it; then have ready laid out on the table a large clean towel or cloth; shake out the starched things lay them on the cloth, and roll it up tightly, and let it remain for three or four hours, when the things will be ready to iron.

IRONING

The irons consist of the common flat-iron, which is of different sizes, varying from 4 to 6 inches in length, triangular in form, and from 2½ to 4½ inches in width at the broad end; the oval iron, which is used for more delicate articles; and the box-iron, which is hollow, and heated by a red-hot iron inserted into the box. The Italian iron is a hollow tube, smooth on the outside, and raised on a slender pedestal with a footstalk. Into the hollow cylinder a red-hot iron is pushed, which heats it; and the smooth outside of the latter is used, on which articles such as frills, and plaited articles are drawn. Crimping and gauffering-machines are used for a kind of plaiting where much regularity is required, the articles being passed through two iron rollers fluted so as to represent the kind of plait or fold required.

It is a good plan to try the heat of the iron on a coarse cloth or apron before ironing anything fine; there is then no danger of scorching. To be able to iron properly requires much practice and experience. Strict cleanliness with all the ironing utensils must be observed, as, if this is not the case, not the most expert ironer will be able to make her things look clear and free from smears &c. After wiping down her ironing-table the laundry-maid should place a coarse cloth on it, and over that the ironing-blanket, with her stand and iron-rubber; and having ascertained that her irons are quite clean and of the right heat, she proceeds with her work. For ironing

AN IRONING
BOARD (RIGHT)
AND GAUFFERING
TONGS (OPPOSITE).
THE TONGS WERE
HEATED AND USED
TO CRISP RUFFLES
AND FRILLS.

fine things, such as collars, cuffs, muslins, and laces, there is nothing so clean and nice to use as the box-iron; the bottom being bright, and never placed near the fire, it is always perfectly clean; it should, however, be kept in a dry place, for fear of it rusting. Gauffering-tongs or irons must be placed in a clear fire for a minute, then withdrawn, wiped with a coarse rubber, and the heat of them tried on a piece of paper, as, unless great care is taken, these will very soon scorch.

The skirts of muslin dresses should be ironed on a skirt-board covered with flannel, and the fronts of shirts on a smaller board, also covered with flannel; this board being placed between the back and front.

After things have been mangled, they should also be ironed in the folds and gathers; dinner-napkins smoothed over, as also table-linen, pillow cases and sometimes sheets. The bands of flannel petticoats, and shoulder-straps to flannel waistcoats, must also undergo the same process.

TO RESTORE WHITENESS TO SCORCHED LINEN

INGREDIENTS
½ *pint of vinegar,*
2 *oz. of fuller's-earth,*
1 *oz. of dried fowls' dung,*
½ *oz. of soap,*
the juice of 2 *large onions.*

———

MODE.—Boil all these ingredients together to the consistency of paste; spread the composition thickly over the damaged part, and if the threads be not actually consumed, after it has been allowed to dry on, and the place has subsequently been washed once or twice, every trace of scorching will disappear.

It was considered
unwholesome tha
other than sleepi
take place in the

mmoral and
any activity,
g, should
edroom...

FAMILY BEDROOMS

I N BED-MAKING, the fancy of its occupant should be consulted: some like beds sloping from the top toward the feet, swelling slightly in the middle; others, perfectly flat; a good housemaid will accommodate each bed to the taste of the sleeper, taking care to shake, beat, and turn it well in the process.

The notion that every room in a Victorian house had its separate function was carried through to the bedroom. It was considered immoral and unwholesome that any activity, other than sleeping, should take place there, and even reading in bed was not encouraged. A bedroom was not a place in which to relax, read or write and it was not for nothing that the 5 o'clock rising bell was instituted in many great houses to herald the beginning of a new day.

In most aristocratic and very wealthy establishments, the master and mistress of the house enjoyed their own apartments, which included separate washing facilities and dressing rooms. The lady of the house sometimes also had a boudoir, or small sitting room, adjoining her bedroom. The words of Mr Francis Place, 'Nothing conduces so much to the degradation of a man and a woman in the opinion of each other than having to perform their separate functions together in the same room' were clearly applauded by the Victorians. The main bedrooms were furnished with a grand four-poster bed, usually of mahogany, with elaborate furnishings and heavily draped curtains. Although the bed had an air of luxury on the surface, with its palliasse, mattress, feather bed and ornate counterpane, two pillows and bolster, it was not constructed for good health or great comfort. It was not until the introduction of the wire-sprung mattress in 1844 that beds became more comfortable to sleep on.

Some persons prefer sleeping on the mattress; in which case a feather bed is usually beneath resting on a second mattress, and a straw palliasse at the bottom. In this case, the mattress should change places daily; the feather bed placed on the mattress shaken, beaten, taken up and opened several times, so as thoroughly to separate the feathers; if too large to be thus handled, the maid should shake and beat one end first, and then the other, smoothing it afterwards equally all over into the required shape, and place the mattress gently over it. The bed-clothes are laid on, beginning with an under blanket and sheet, which are tucked under the mattress at the bottom. The bolster is then beaten and shaken, and put on, the top of the sheet rolled around it, and the sheet tucked in all round. The pillows and other bed-clothes follow, and the counterpane over all, which should fall in graceful folds.

Other furnishings included a large mahogany wardrobe, fitted with drawers and shelves for every specific article of clothing, including a long hanging space with hooks or pegs; coat hangers, or 'shoulders', as they were known, were not in general use until much later. There were deep drawers for hats and bonnets and shallow ones for gloves and handkerchiefs, usually lined in pretty paper, and one or two long mirrors, either hung on the inside of the doors, or as part of the exterior decoration.

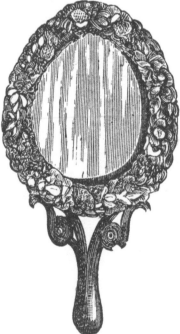

An important piece of furniture was a single or double washstand, with a marble top and a set of washstand ware and matching crockery. The washstand sometimes had towel rails attached to the side or there would be a separate, free-standing towel holder. There was usually a mahogany dressing table groaning with accoutrements, including a set of brushes, a tray, a ring stand, bottles, several china pots and jars, plenty of knick-knacks and all the other paraphernalia with which the Victorians loved to surround themselves, and in the middle of all this was a dressing-glass. Another popular piece was the cheval glass, which was a

free-standing long mirror with castors concealed in the feet, and sometimes brass or bronzed candle-branches on either side.

 No bedroom was complete without its chamber pot and there were several ways in which these were housed. They were concealed in various places, sometimes in a small cupboard under the washstand or in a chair called a commode. Others were hidden in a bed cupboard or in a set of bed-steps, with two steps arranged as cupboards. The tread of the top step was hinged and lifted up and the middle step pulled forwards with a lid that lifted up with space for a bidet or other conveniences. When there were steps of this kind on either side of the bed, the middle step of one would hold a night convenience and the other a bidet.

 There were always several chairs, one or two serving as bedside tables as these, as we know them today, were not part of Victorian bedroom furniture. Before bathrooms became commonplace, there was generally a hip-bath in the dressing room, or in the bedroom,

[*213*]

hidden behind a moveable screen or curtain. Bathrooms, as we think of them today, did not exist in Mrs Beeton's time and regular bathing was often considered a threat to increasing disease, with cold or tepid water being the order of the day, even for young children. It was not unfashionable to be dirty and one royal duke was heard to say that sweat kept a man clean. Some people, however, such as Beau Brummel, arbiter of taste, preferred cleanliness to highly scented dirt. Arthur Wellesley (later Duke of Wellington) was considered somewhat outré in that he took a daily bath. By the end of Mrs Beeton's life, daily baths were fashionable with the upper classes, but most middle-class households were still content with a daily wash, using a basin and jug of water in the bedroom, and a weekly bath.

As there was no other means of heating, bedrooms were often very cold at night once the fire had died down, and most people slept in nightcaps and bed-socks, with at least four layers of blankets. In many great houses, a coal-man would patrol the corridors at night calling out "coal" and those night-owls who were still awake would usher him in to replenish their fire.

Victorians were preoccupied with making a good outward impression, but when it came to rooms that were not seen by others, it was a different story and they were very frugal wherever possible. The corridors, with no heating, were freezing in winter and to get from the downstairs rooms to the bedrooms was never a pleasant experience.

EWERS AND
BASINS WERE THE
ONLY WASHING
FACILITIES IN
VICTORIAN
BEDROOMS. THE
EWERS WERE
FILLED BY THE
HOUSEMAIDS.

Children's bedrooms

Not a great deal of attention was
paid to the furnishings of
children's rooms, as a child's
bedroom in most houses was
only used for sleeping and
dressing. Most of the furniture
consisted of cast-off pieces that
were considered no longer good
enough for the public rooms
downstairs. Odd tables and
chairs that were out of fashion, a
worn rug, a small utility bed and
a cupboard for their clothes were
the order of the day. Children's
bedrooms were situated at the
top of the house, well away from
their parents and the entertainment areas. When very young they
bathed, slept, played and took their meals in the nursery, watched over
by the nursery-maid. Once they were old enough to attend the school
room and the boys were sent away to boarding school, boys and girls
were segregated, but, depending on how many children there were,
it could often be three or four to one room.

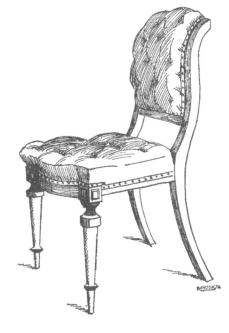

CHAIRS WERE
OFTEN USED AS
BEDSIDE TABLES AS
WELL AS SEATS.

Children were strictly regimented by their minders and generally
played an insignificant role in the adult household. They were taught
to be seen and not heard and only very rarely did parents in grand
establishments ever visit their children's bedrooms. Adolescent
girls' bedrooms gradually became more feminine and full of typical
Victorian bits and pieces, while the boys' rooms were often austere,
only being used during school holidays. Children's bedrooms were
often cold, as Victorians believed heating was not good for the health
and constitution of children. In many paintings and engravings of
the time, children were shown wearing coats and boots as they went
to and from their bedrooms.

A servant is not to
or wear a hat in th
mistress's presen
any opinion, unle

e seated
house, in her
; nor offer
asked for it...

THE LADY'S MAID

THE LADY'S-MAID, from her supposed influence with her mistress, is exposed to some temptations to which other servants are less subjected. She is probably in communication with the tradespeople who supply articles for the toilet; such as hatters, dressmakers and perfumers. The conduct of waiting-maid to these people should be civil but independent, making reasonable allowance for want of exact punctuality, and if any such can be made, she should represent any inconvenience respectfully, and if an excuse seems unreasonable, put the matter fairly to the mistress, leaving it up to her to notice it further, if she thinks it necessary. No expectations of a personal character should influence her one way or the other. It would be acting unreasonably to any domestic to make her refuse such presents as tradespeople choose to give her; the utmost that can be expected is that they should not influence her judgement in the articles supplied—that she should represent them truly to the mistress without fear and without favour. Civility to all, servility to none, is a good maxim for every one.

Deference to a mistress, and to her friends and visitors, is one of the implied terms of their engagement; and this deference must apply even to what may be considered her whims. A servant is not to be seated or wear a hat in the house, in her mistress's presence; nor offer any opinion, unless asked for it; nor even to say "good night" or "good morning", except in reply to that situation.

> Not all Victorian ladies were in a position to have their own personal maid and it was usually only the aristocracy, or a very wealthy household that could run to such luxury. In many cases the mistress would have her favourite housemaid to assist her, one she could trust not to gossip too much to the other servants. Usually the mistress herself would interview

A LADY'S
MAID WAS HER
MISTRESS'S
CLOSEST SERVANT.

all prospective personal maids rather than leaving it to the house-keeper to choose one for her. This particular maid needed a great deal of discretion and loyalty to her mistress, and at no time should she discuss private matters she may be privileged to hear or see. Strict etiquette was observed by the servants and in most households the lady's maid was allowed a seat at the housekeeper's table.

DUTIES OF A LADY'S-MAID

The duties of a lady's-maid are more numerous, and perhaps more onerous, than that of the valet; for while the latter is aided by the tailor, the hatter, the linen-draper, and the perfumer; the lady's-maid has to originate many parts of the mistress's dress herself: she should, indeed, be a tolerably expert milliner and dressmaker, a good hairdresser, and possess some chemical knowledge of the cosmetics with which the toilet-table is supplied, in order to use them with safety and effect.

Her first duty in the morning, after having performed her own toilet, is to examine the clothes put off by her mistress the evening before, either to put them away, or to see that they are all in order to put on again. During the winter, and in wet weather, the dresses should be carefully examined, and the mud removed. Dresses of tweed, and other woollen materials, may be laid out on a table and brushed all over; but in general, even in woollen fabrics, the light-ness of the tissues renders brushing unsuitable to dresses, and it is better to remove the dust from the folds by beating them lightly with a handkerchief or thin cloth. Silk dresses should never be brushed, but rubbed with a piece of merino, or other soft material, of a similar colour, kept for the purpose. Summer dresses of barège, muslin, mohair, and other light materials, simply require shaking;

A LADY'S MAID
WAS SUPPOSED TO
HAVE THE UTMOST
DISCRETION. BUT
THIS MAID SEEMS
UNABLE TO RESIST
A PEAK AT HER
MISTRESS'S
LETTER AS SHE
DRESSES HER HAIR.

A MISTRESS
EXPECTED HER
MAID TO HELP HER
DRESS AND
ARRANGE HER
CLOTHING.

but if the muslin be tumbled, it must be ironed afterwards. If the dresses require slight repair, it should be done at once: 'a stitch in time saves nine.'

These various preliminary offices performed, the lady's-maid should prepare for dressing her mistress, arranging her dressing-room, toilet-table, and linen, according to her mistress's wishes and habits. The details of dressing we need not touch upon,—every lady has her own mode of doing so; but the maid should move about quietly, perform any offices about her mistress's person, as lacing stays, gently, and adjust her linen smoothly.

Having prepared the dressing-room by lighting the fire, sweeping the hearth, and made everything ready for dressing her mistress, placed her linen before the fire to air, and laid out the various articles of dress she is to wear, which will probably have been arranged the previous evening, the lady's-maid is prepared for the morning's duties.

> If there were several daughters in the household, they would sometimes each have their own maid, or share one between them, depending on the wealth and position of the family in society. In more modest establishments where there may be only one or two maids to cope with all the household duties, any extra tasks for the mistress would fall on the already overworked, underpaid and often very young housemaid.

FURTHER TASKS

Having dressed her mistress for breakfast, and breakfasted herself, the further duties of the lady's-maid will depend altogether upon the habits of the family, in which hardly two will probably agree. Where the duties are entirely confined to attendance of her mistress, it is probable that the bed-room and dressing-room will be committed to her care; that the housemaid will rarely enter, except for the weekly or other periodical cleaning; she will, therefore, have to make her mistress's bed, and keep it in order; and as her duties are light and easy, there can be no allowance made for the slightest approach to uncleanliness or want of order.

Every morning, immediately after her mistress has left it, and while breakfast is on, she should throw the bed open, by taking off the clothes; open the window (except in rainy weather) and leave the room to air for half an hour.

After breakfast, except her attendance on her mistress prevents it, if the rooms are carpeted, she should sweep them carefully, having previously strewed the room with moist tea-leaves, dusting every table and chair, taking care to penetrate to every corner, and moving every article of furniture that is portable. This done satisfactorily, and having cleaned the dressing-glass, polished up the furniture and the ornaments, and made the glass jug and basin clean and bright, emptied all slops, emptied the water-jugs and filled them with fresh water, and arranged the rooms, the dressing-room is ready for the mistress when she thinks proper to appear.

The dressing-room thoroughly in order, the same thing is to be done in the bedroom, in which she will probably be assisted by a housemaid to make the bed and empty the slops. In making the bed, she will study her lady's wishes, whether it is to be hard or soft, sloping or straight, and see that it is done accordingly. Having swept the bedroom with equal care, dusted the tables and chairs, chimney-ornaments, and put away all articles of dress left from yesterday, and cleaned and put away any articles of jewellery, her next care is to see, before her mistress goes out, what requires replacing in her department, and furnish her with a list of them, that she may use her discretion about ordering them. All this done, she may settle herself down to any work on which she is engaged. This will consist chiefly in mending, which is first to be seen to; everything, except stockings, being mended before washing. Plain work will probably be one of the lady's-maid chief employments.

The evening duties of a lady's-maid are pretty nearly a repetition of those of the morning. She is in attendance when her mistress retires; she assists her to undress if required, brushes her hair, and renders such other assistance as is demanded; removes all slops; takes care that the fire, if any, is safe, before she retires to rest herself.

CARING FOR
THE MISTRESS'S CLOTHES

Among other duties, the lady's-maid should understand the various processes for washing, and cleaning, and repairing laces; edging of collars; removing stains and grease-spots from dresses, and similar processes.

The bonnet should be dusted with a light feather plume, in order to remove every particle of dust. Velvet bonnets, and other velvet articles of dress, should be cleaned with a soft brush. If the flowers with which the bonnet is decorated have been crushed or misplaced, or the leaves tumbled, they should be raised and readjusted by means of flower pliers. If feathers have suffered from damp, they should be held near the fire for a few minutes, and restored to their

A MAID HAD
CHARGE OF HER
MISTRESS'S
JEWELLERY AND
HELPED HER PUT
THE FINISHING
TOUCHES TO HER
ENSEMBLE.

[*225*]

PRESERVATIVES AGAINST
THE RAVAGES OF MOTHS

PLACE pieces of camphor, cedar-wood, Russia leather, tobacco-leaves, bog-myrtle, or anything else strongly aromatic, in the drawers or boxes where furs or other things to be preserved from moths are kept, and they will never take harm.

natural state by the hand or a soft brush, or recurled with a blunt knife dipped in very hot water.

The Chausserie, or foot-gear of a lady, is one of the few things left to mark her station, and requires special care. Satin boots or shoes should be dusted with a soft brush, or wiped with a cloth. Kid or varnished leather should have the mud wiped off with a sponge charged with milk, which preserves its softness and polish. Ironing is a part of the duties of a lady's maid, and she should be able to do it in the most perfect manner when it becomes necessary. Ironing is

IRONING HAD TO
BE DONE WITH
THE UTMOST CARE
TO AVOID DAMAGE
TO A LADY'S
EXPENSIVE GOWNS.
ALL EQUIPMENT
HAD TO BE
PERFECTLY CLEAN.
OPPOSITE IS A
DRESS STAND.

THE CARE OF THE HAIR

TO MAKE POMADE FOR THE HAIR

—

INGREDIENTS.
¼ lb. of lard,
2 pennyworth of castor-oil;
scent.

—

MODE. – Let the lard be unsalted; beat it up well; then add the castor-oil, and mix thoroughly together with a knife, adding a few drops of any scent that may be preferred. Put the pomatum into pots, which keep well covered to prevent it turning rancid.

TO MAKE BANDOLINE

—

INGREDIENTS.
1oz. of gum-tragacanth,
¼ pint of cold water,
3 pennyworth of essence of almonds,
2 teaspoons of old rum.

—

MODE. – Put the gum-tragacanth into a wide-mouthed bottle with the cold water; let it stand until dissolved, then stir into it the essence of almonds; let it remain for an hour or two, then pour the rum on the top. This should make the stock bottle, and when any is required for use, it is merely necessary to dilute it with a little cold water until the desired consistency is obtained, and to keep it in a small bottle, well corked, for use. This bandoline, instead of injuring the hair, as many other kinds often do, improves it, by increasing its growth, and making it always smooth and glossy.

TO PROMOTE THE GROWTH OF HAIR

—

INGREDIENTS.
Equal quantities of olive oil
and spirit of rosemary;
a few drops of oil of nutmeg.

—

MODE. – Mix the ingredients together, rub the roots of the hair every night with a little of this liniment, and the growth of it will very soon sensibly increase. When illness is the cause of the loss of hair, brandy should be applied three times a week, and cold cream on the alternate nights.

A GOOD WASH FOR THE HAIR

—

INGREDIENTS.
1 pennyworth of borax,
½ pint of olive oil,
1 pint of boiling water.

—

MODE. – Pour the boiling water over the borax and oil; let it cool; then put the mixture into a bottle. Shake it before using, and apply it with a flannel.

Camphor and borax, dissolved in boiling water and left to cool, make a very good wash for the hair; as also does rosemary-water mixed with a little borax.

After using any of these washes, when the hair becomes thoroughly dry, a little pomatum or oil should be rubbed in, to make it smooth and glossy.

often badly done from inattention to a few very simple requirements. Cleanliness is the first essential: the ironing-board, the fire,
the iron, and the ironing-blanket should all be perfectly clean.

Hairdressing is the most important part of the lady's-maid's
office. Lessons in hairdressing may be obtained, and at not an
unreasonable charge. If a lady's maid can afford it, we would advise
her to initiate herself in the mysteries of hairdressing before entering on her duties. If a mistress finds her maid handy, and willing to

DESIGN FOR A COTTAGE

learn, she will not mind the expense of a few lessons, which are most necessary, as the fashion and mode of dressing the hair is continually changing. Brushes and combs should be kept scrupulously clean, by washing them about twice a week: to do this oftener spoils the brushes, as very frequent washing makes them so very soft.

A waiting-maid, who wishes to make herself useful, will study the fashion-books with attention, so as to be able to aid her mistress's judgement in dressing, according to the prevailing fashion, with such modifications as her style of countenance requires. She will also, if she has her mistress's interest at heart, employ her spare time in repairing and making up dresses which have served one purpose, to serve another also; or turning many things, unfitted for her mistress to use, for the younger branches of the family. The lady's-maid may thus render herself invaluable to her mistress, and increase her own happiness in so doing. The exigencies of fashion and luxury are such, that all ladies, except those of the very highest rank, will consider themselves fortunate in having about them a thoughtful person, capable of diverting their finery to a useful purpose.

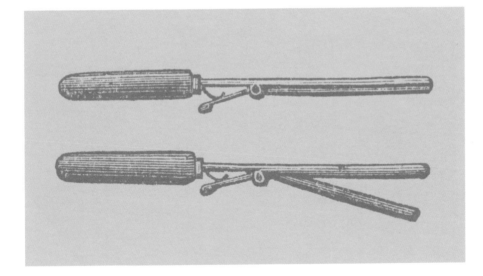

CURLING IRONS
SUCH AS THESE
WERE PART OF THE
ARMOURY OF
EQUIPMENT USED
BY THE LADY'S
MAID TO BEAUTIFY
HER MISTRESS.

TRAVELLING WITH THE MISTRESS

Ladies who keep a waiting-maid for their own persons are in the habit of paying visits to their friends, in which it is not unusual for the maid to accompany them; at all events, it is her duty to pack the trunks; and this requires not only knowledge but some practice, although the improved trunks and portmanteaus now made, in which there is a place for nearly everything, render this more simple than formerly. Before packing, let the trunks be thoroughly cleaned, and, if necessary, lined with paper, and everything intended for packing laid on the bed or chairs, so that it may be seen what is to be stowed away; the nicer articles of dress neatly folded in clean calico wrappers. Having satisfied herself that everything wanted is laid out, and that it is in perfect order, the packing is commenced by disposing of the most bulky articles, the dressing-case and work-box, skirts, and other articles requiring room, leaving the smaller articles

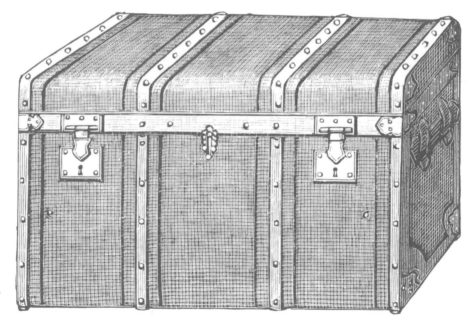

THE LADY'S MAID
WAS RESPONSIBLE
FOR PACKING ALL
THAT WAS NEEDED
WHEN HER
MISTRESS WENT TO
VISIT FRIENDS.

to fill up; finally, having satisfied herself that all is included, she
should lock and cover up the trunk in its canvas case, and then pack
her own box, if she is to accompany her mistress.

On reaching the house, the lady's-maid will be shown her lady's
apartment; and her duties here are what they were at home; she will
arrange her mistress's things, and learn which is her bell, in order to
go to her when she rings. Her meals will be taken in the housekeeper's room; and here she must be discreet and guarded in her
talk to any one of her mistress or her concerns. Her only occupation
here will be attending in her lady's room, keeping her things in
order, and making her rooms comfortable for her.

It is no wonder the lady's maid needed to 'possess some chemical
knowledge of the cosmetics with which the toilet-table is supplied,
in order to use them with safety and effect'. It is also no wonder the
Victorians slept in nightcaps if they used any of the recipes on page
228 regularly. Pomade was a scented ointment for application to
the skin, now used especially for the skin of the head and the hair.
Bandoline was a gummy preparation for fixing the hair when styling.

CARING FOR JEWELLERY

JEWELS are generally wrapped up
in cotton, and kept in their cases;
but they are subject to tarnish from
exposure to the air, and require
cleaning. This is done by preparing
clean soap-suds, using fine toilet-
soap. Dip any article of gold, silver,
gilt, or precious stones into this lye,
and dry them by brushing with a
brush of soft badgers' hair, or a fine
sponge; afterwards with a piece of
fine cloth, and, lastly, with a soft
leather.

No man is a he

to his valet...

THE VALET

ATTENDANTS ON THE PERSON—"No man is a hero to his valet," saith the proverb; and the corollary may run, "No lady is a heroine to her maid." The infirmities are, perhaps, too numerous and too equally distributed to stand the severe microscopic tests which attendants on the person have opportunities of applying. The valet and waiting-maid are placed near the persons of the master and mistress, receiving orders only from them, dressing them, accompanying them in all their journeys, the confidants and agents of their most unguarded moments, of their most secret habits, and of course subject to their commands,—even to their caprices; they themselves being subject to erring judgement, aggravated by an imperfect education. All that can be expected from such servants is polite manners, modest demeanour, and a respectful reserve, which are indispensable. To these, good sense, good temper, some self-denial, and consideration for the feelings of others, whether above or below them in the social scale, will be useful qualifications. Their duty leads them to wait on those who are, from sheer wealth, station, and education, more polished, and consequently more susceptible of annoyance; and any vulgar familiarity of manner is opposed to all their notions of self-respect. Quiet unobtrusive manners, therefore, and a delicate reserve in speaking of their employers, either in praise or blame, is as essential in their absence, as good manners and respectful conduct in their presence.

The valet was usually found only in establishments of the aristocracy or the very wealthy. A valet's employer was required to pay an annual tax of one guinea a year, as the Treasury regarded men servants as a luxury.

[*237*]

An exemption to this rule was permitted for elderly or disabled naval and military officers and they were allowed to employ one manservant free of tax. In these circumstances, the valet often slept in his master's room, or very close by and was something of a minder, as well as being a companion and dresser. He would also carry out any secretarial duties required.

A VALET'S DUTIES

His day commences by seeing that his master's dressing-room is in order; that the housemaid has swept and dusted it properly; that the fire is lighted and burns cheerfully; and some time before his master is expected, he will do well to throw up the sash to admit fresh air, closing it, however, in time to recover the temperature which he knows his master prefers. It is now his duty to place the body-linen on the horse before the fire, to be aired properly; to lay the trousers

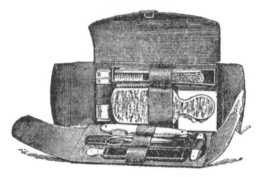

A VALET'S BOX,
CONTAINING
BRUSHES AND
OTHER GROOMING
EQUIPMENT.

intended to be worn, carefully brushed and cleaned, on the back of his master's chair; while the coat and waistcoat, carefully brushed and folded, and the collar cleaned, are laid in their place ready to put on when required. All the articles of the toilet should be in their places, the razors properly set and stropped, and hot water ready for use.

Gentlemen generally prefer performing the operation of shaving themselves, but a valet should be prepared to do it if required; and he should besides, be a good hairdresser. Shaving over, he has to

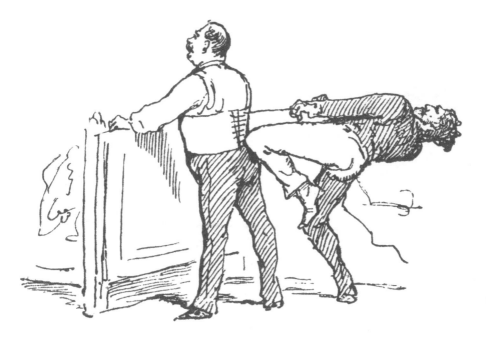

brush the hair, beard and moustache, where that appendage is encouraged, arranging the whole simply and gracefully, according to the age and style of countenance. Every fortnight, or three weeks at the utmost, the hair should be cut, and the points of the whiskers trimmed as often as required. A good valet will now present the various articles of the toilet as they are wanted; afterwards, the body-linen, neck-tie, which he will put on, if required, and afterwards, waistcoat, coat, and boots, in suitable order, and carefully brushed and polished.

Having thus seen his master dressed, if he is about to go out, the valet will hand him his cane, gloves, and hat, the latter well brushed on the outside with a soft brush, and wiped inside with a clean handkerchief, respectfully attend him to the door, and open it for him, and receive his last orders for the day. Now he proceeds to put everything in order in the dressing-room, cleans the combs and brushes, and brushes and folds up any clothes that may be left about the room, and puts them away in the drawers.

It is, perhaps, unnecessary to add that, having discharged all the

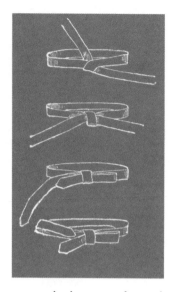

commissions intrusted to him by his master, such as conveying notes or messages to friends, or the tradesmen, all of which he should punctually and promptly attend to, it is his duty to be waiting when his master returns home to dress for dinner, or for any other reason, and to have all things prepared for this second dressing. Previous to this, he brings under his notice the cards of visitors who may have called, delivers the messages he may have received for him, and otherwise acquits himself of the morning's commissions, and receives his orders for the remainder of the day. The routine of his evening duty is to have the dressing-room and study, where there is a separate one, arranged comfortably for his master, the fires lighted, candles prepared, dressing-gown and slippers in their place, and aired, and everything in order that is required for his master's comforts.

Not many married men had a valet. Valets were usually employed by bachelors living away from home, either in up-market lodgings or at their exclusive 'clubs for gentlemen'. No matter how close the valet was to his master, he had always to treat him with deference and respect, never letting his personal feelings show and never taking for granted his special position of trust. He had to be discreet at all times and never acquire ideas above his station.

A VALET'S DUTIES INCLUDED TAKING CARE OF HIS MASTER'S COLLARS (ABOVE) AS WELL AS CARING FOR HIS CLOTHES AND EVEN MAKING TRAVEL ARRANGEMENTS.

POLISHING BOOTS

Polish for the boots is an important matter to the valet, and not always to be obtained good by purchase; never so good, perhaps, as he can make for himself after the following recipe: Take of ivory-black and treacle each 4oz., Sulphuric acid 1oz., best olive-oil 2 spoonfuls, best white-wine vinegar 3 half-pints: mix the ivory-black and treacle well in an earthen jar; then add the sulphuric acid, continuing to stir the mixture; next pour in the oil; and lastly add the vinegar, stirring it in by degrees, until thoroughly incorporated.

Another polish is made by mixing 1oz each of pounded galls and logwood-chips, and 3lbs. of red French wine (ordinaire). Boil together till the liquid is reduced to half the quantity, and pour it off through a strainer. Now take ½ pound each of pounded gum-arabic and lump sugar, 1oz of green copperas, and 3lbs of brandy. Dissolve the gum-arabic in the previous decoction, and add the sugar and copperas: when all is dissolved and mixed together, stir in the brandy, mixing it smoothly. This mixture will yield 5 or 6 lbs of a very superior polishing paste for boots and shoes.

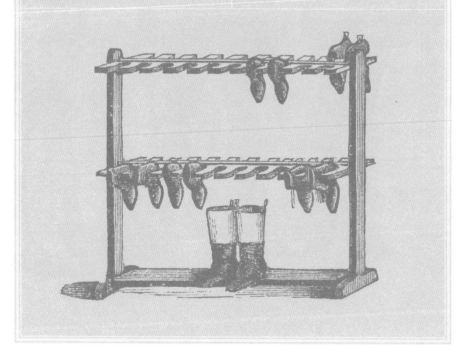

Gentlemen are sometimes in-different as to their clothes and appearance; it is the valet's duty, in this case, where his master permits it, to select from the wardrobe such things as are suitable for the occasion, so that he may appear with scrupulous neatness and cleanliness; that his linen and neck-tie, where that is white or coloured, are unsoiled; and where he is not accustomed to change them every day, that the cravat is turned, and even ironed, to remove the crease of the previous fold. The coat collar,—which, where the hair is oily and worn long, is apt to get greasy—should also be examined; a careful valet will correct this by removing the spots day by day as they appear, first by mois-tening the grease-spots with a little rectified spirits of wine or spirits of hartshorn, which has a renovating effect, and the smell of which soon disappears. The grease is dissolved and removed by gentle scraping. The grease removed, add a little more of the spirit, and rub it with the palm of the hand, in the direction of the grain of the cloth, and it will be clean and glossy as the rest of the garment.

A VALET USED A HAT IRON (ABOVE) AND CLOTHES BRUSHES (BELOW) IN THE CARE OF HIS MASTER'S CLOTHES.

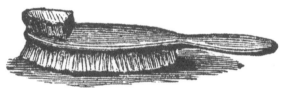

The nurse must l
clean and tidy in l
Snuff-taking and
must not be inclu

scrupulously

r person…

irit-drinking

d in her habits.

THE NURSERY
& SCHOOLROOM

THE NURSERY is of great importance in every family, and in families of distinction, where there are several young children, it is an establishment kept apart from the rest of the family, under the charge of an upper nurse, assisted by under nursery-maids proportioned to the work to be done. The responsible duties of the upper nursemaid commences with the weaning of the child: it must now be separated from the mother or wet-nurse, at least for a time, and the cares of the nursemaid, which have hitherto been only occasionally put in requisition, are now to be entirely devoted to the infant. She washes, dresses and feeds it; walks out

with it, and regulates all its little wants; and, even at this early age, many good qualities are required to do so in a satisfactory manner. Patience and good temper are indispensable qualities; truthfulness, purity of manners, minute cleanliness, and docility and obedience, almost equally so. She ought also to be acquainted with the art of ironing and trimming little caps, and be handy with her needle.

The concept of a nursery was quite a new idea as J.C. Loudon explains in his book, *An Encyclopaedia of Cottage, Farm and Villa Architecture and Furniture*, published in 1833, but within 25 years it had become standard in most houses. In larger establishments there would have been a night nursery for sleeping and a day room for meals, play and lessons.

In upper middle-class homes the nursery was situated at the top of the house near to the servants' quarters. This segregated the children from the adults, but made access difficult for the parents and meant that carrying supplies up and down stairs several times a day was heavy work for the servants. One other observation about this comes from *Our Homes, and How to Make them Healthy*, published in 1883, in which the author warns that there should not be sinks on the same floor as the nursery as 'The manifest convenience of having a sink near to rid the nursery department of soiled water has to be weighed against the tendency of all servants to misuse such convenience, and it is best to decide against such sources of mischief'. No wonder nurseries were whitewashed or distempered every year.

In the grandest establishments there were sometimes three nursery staff: the upper nurse, who was assisted by an under nursery-maid and often a wet-nurse. In more modest houses of the new middle class there was often only one nursery nurse. This female needed to have the constitution of an ox, the patience of Job and the medical skills of Florence Nightingale, if she was to meet the demanding requirements of her job set out by Mrs Beeton.

The under nursemaid lights the fires, sweeps, scours and dusts the rooms, and makes the beds; empties slops, and carries up water; brings up and removes the nursery meals; washes and dresses all the children, except the infant, and assists in mending. Where there is a

BATHTIME
IN FRONT OF
THE NURSERY FIRE
FOR THIS NURSE-
MAID'S YOUNGEST
CHARGE.

nursery girl to assist, she does the
rougher part of the cleaning; and all
take their meals in the nursery together,
after the children of the family have
done.

In smaller families, where there is
only one nursemaid kept, she is assisted
by the housemaid, or servant-of-all-
work, who will do the rougher part of
the work and carry up the nursery
meals. In such circumstances she will be
more immediately under the eye of her
mistress, who will probably relieve her
from some of the cares of her infant.

Where the nurse has the entire
charge of the nursery, and the mother is
too much occupied to do more than pay
a daily visit to it, it is desirable that she
be a person of observation, and possess
some acquaintance with the diseases
incident to childhood, as also with such
simple remedies as may be useful before a medical attendant can be
procured, or where such attendance is not considered necessary.

All these little ailments are preceded by symptoms so minute as
to be only perceptible to close observation; such as twitching of the
brows, restless sleep, grinding the gums, and, in some inflammatory
diseases, even to the child abstaining from crying, from fear of the
increased pain produced by the movement. Dentition, or cutting
the teeth, is attended with many of these symptoms. Measles,
thrush, scarlatina, croup, hooping-cough, and other childish complaints, are all preceded by well-known symptoms, which may be

MANY AN INFANT
SPENT MORE TIME
WITH ITS NURSE
THAN ITS MOTHER.

alleviated and rendered less virulent by simple remedies instantaneously applied.

She must be scrupulously clean and tidy in her person, honest, sober, and noiseless in her movements; should possess a natural love of children and have strong nerve in case of emergencies. Snuff-taking and spirit-drinking must not be included in her habits. In higher families, the upper nurse is usually permitted to sup or dine occasionally at the housekeeper's table by way of relaxation, when the children are all well, and her subordinates trustworthy.

J. C. Loudon describes the furnishings of the nursery. 'The first piece of furniture which an infant can be said to use is a bassinet, or portable bed. It is two feet and a half long, the frame of which is made of wickerwork, with a hood which falls backwards or forwards as required. It is generally lined with printed furniture or sometimes with dimity, to keep out the draught. The hood is covered with furniture and two little curtains drop down from its front, which are looped up with tapes or ribands in the manner as tent-

A RANGE
OF DIFFERENT
INFANT CRIBS WAS
AVAILABLE, SUCH
AS THIS BABY
BASKET (ABOVE)
AND THE
BERCEAUNETTE
(RIGHT).

bed furniture. A hair mattress stuffed very soft, and a small down pillow complete the bed. The child may also be removed in it from one room to another without being disturbed. A mother will find such a bed particularly useful in the evening when the child is asleep beside her in the sitting room; because it need not be disturbed, but may be carried in the bassinet to the bedroom, and there be placed by the side of the bed; whereas, if the child were asleep on a sofa, its removal, by taking it up in the arms, would be certain to awake it, and the mother might lose her rest for several hours.'

Next is the crib which is 'a bedstead for children so young as to render it unsafe to trust them by themselves in beds with unguarded sides. They are generally intended to be placed, during the night, by the bedside of the mother; and for that purpose, the height of the crib should correspond with that of the large bed, and one of its sides to lift out.'

At this time there were about four popular chairs on the market in London. 'A child's chair of the first kind, having a night pan, and a matted seat. A small stuffed flannel of the size of the seat, and having a round hole in the centre, is generally placed over it when it is to be used, in order to prevent the pan from hurting the child. In England, infants of ordinary health and strength are put into chairs of this kind, when between three and four months.'

Next was a child's high chair which is 'to be used when it first begins to sit at table. There is a bar or stick put across between the arms, to keep the child from falling out, and sometimes there is a foot-board. A child in average health is put in such a chair when between twelve or fourteen months.'

There was a child's 'elbow-chair, or bergere, as it was commonly called in England. This chair stands on a stool, to which it is attached by a thumb-screw; and when the chair is removed from the stool, the latter forms a table for the child to put its playthings on. The shelf for the feet is made to move higher or lower as may be required. The chair is only fixed on the stool when the child is to sit at table to eat, which it

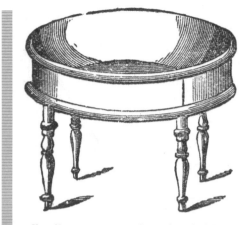

may do when about eighteen months of age.'

One rather dangerous looking chair was called an 'Astley Cooper's chair; being recommended by that eminent surgeon, with the view of preventing children from acquiring a habit of leaning forward, or stooping; the upright position of the back affording support when the child is placed at table, and eating, which a sloping-backed chair does not. It is proper to observe that some medical men do not approve of these chairs.'

All nurseries had washing facilities and one very popular design was 'a child's washing-stand, consisting of a table about eighteen inches high, with a large basin and a soap cup sunk in one side of the top. The table is made lower than a chair, in order that the nurse may have the more power over the child when she is washing it. When the child is only a few weeks old, it is immersed, or bathed in the basin; but as it grows larger, it sits on the top of the table, with its legs in the water.'

There was usually a large solid central table and chairs for meals and lessons and a large toy cupboard. The floor would have a rug which would be taken up and beaten at least once a week and a high mesh fire guard in front of the grate. This was foremost as a safety precaution, but it was also useful as a place on which damp clothes could be aired.'

A BABY BATH
(ABOVE) AND A
HIGH FIRE GUARD
WERE
ESSENTIALS FOR
THE NURSERY.

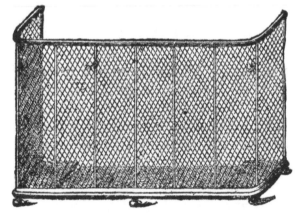

CHILDREN
PLAYING A FOR-
FEIT GAME CALLED
'HATCHET'.

CARE OF THE CHILD

There is a considerable art in carrying an infant comfortably for itself and for the nursemaid. If she carry it always upright on her arm, and presses it too closely against her chest, the stomach of the child is apt to get compressed, and the back fatigued. For her own comfort, a good nurse will frequently vary this position, by changing from one arm to the other, and sometimes by laying it across both, raising the head a little.

When teaching it to walk, and guiding it by the hand, she should change the hand from time to time, so as to avoid raising one shoulder higher than the other. This is the only way in which a child should be taught to walk; leading-strings and other foolish inventions, which force an infant to make efforts, with its shoulders and head forward, before it knows how to use its limbs, will only render it feeble, and retard its progress.

[*253*]

The average number of children in a middle-class Victorian household was between five and six and they were brought up to be early risers, as lying in bed was said to be not only lazy, but also sinful. Once they had all been washed and dressed, breakfast was brought up from the kitchen, and the morning routine would begin. There was playtime for the little ones when sometimes the mistress would visit the nursery to read to them or help the girls with their sewing. The older ones would have lessons from the governess until lunch, which was again served in the nursery. After lunch the younger children would have a short sleep, followed by a walk in the park.

After the walk the children were washed and dressed to be taken downstairs to see their parents for about an hour. During which, if they were old enough, they would make polite conversation, play a musical instrument, recite or just sit quietly and listen attentively, without fidgeting or interrupting. All Victorian children were taught very early on in life to know their place. They would then return upstairs to the nursery where they would have tea and be allowed to play until it was time to be washed and sent to bed.

MOST CHILDREN SPENT AN HOUR WITH THEIR MOTHER IN THE AFTERNOON.

Most children have some bad habit, of which they must be broken; but this is never accomplished by harshness without developing worse evils; kindness, perseverance, and patience in the nurse, are here of the utmost importance. When finger-sucking is one of these habits, the fingers are sometimes rubbed with bitter aloes, or some equally disagreeable substance. Others have dirty habits, which are only to be changed with patience, perseverance, and, above all, by regularity in the nurse. She should never be permitted to inflict punishment on these occasions, or, indeed, on any occasion. But, if punishment is to be avoided, it is still more necessary that all kinds of

indulgences and flattery be equally forbidden.

Yielding to all the whims of a child,—picking up its toys when thrown away in mere wantonness, would be intolerable. A child should never be led to think others inferior to it, to beat a dog, or even the stone against which it falls, as some children are taught to do by silly nurses. Neither should the nurse affect or show alarm at any of the little accidents which must inevitably happen; if it falls, treat it as a trifle; otherwise she encourages a spirit of cowardice and timidity. But she will take care that such accidents are not of frequent occurrence, or the result of neglect.

Nurseries of the middle and upper classes were well stocked with toys. The wooden rocking horse was a great favourite and there was always a doll's house for the girls, complete with a set of miniature furniture. Every little girl possessed several beautiful Victorian dolls, which were made with heads and shoulders of china, bisque or wax with moulded composition or stuffed calico bodies. They were usually beautifully dressed as adults in the latest fashions. The boys would have their collections of lead or tin soldiers. The older children would often have a toy theatre, usually made from card, which stood on a table and had characters and scenes printed on card or paper. One of the most popular toys was a Noah's Ark, which was there not only to be played with, but also to teach the children the story of the flood. In most strict Victorian households this was the only toy they were allowed to play with on Sundays.

The nurse should keep the child as clean as possible, and particularly she should train it to habits of cleanliness, so that it should feel uncomfortable when otherwise; watching especially that it does not soil itself in eating.

At the same time, vanity in its personal appearance is not to be encouraged by over-care in this respect, or by too tight lacing or buttoning of dresses, nor a small foot cultivation by use of tight shoes. If a child is sick, selfish and thoughtless nurses, and mothers too, must not yield to giving cordials and sleeping-draughts, whose effects are too well known.

Nursemaids would do well to repeat to the parents faithfully and truly the defects they observe in the dispositions of very young children. If properly checked in time, evil propensities may be eradicated; but this should not extend to anything but serious defects; or otherwise, the intuitive perceptions which all children possess will

GAMES SUCH AS
BLIND MAN'S
BUFF WERE
POPULAR WITH
THE YOUNGER
CHILDREN IN
THE HOUSE.

construe the act into "spying" and "informing" which should never be resorted to in the case of children, nor, indeed, in any case'.

At the end of the chapter on the duties of the nursemaids, Mrs Beeton includes remedies for such childhood ailments as Dentition (teething), Chilblains and Worms, as well as the serious, and sometimes fatal Croup, which recommends the use of 'one or two leeches to applied to the throat should the symptoms remain unabated after a few hours'.

* * *

Although Mrs Beeton has very little to say on the subject of the schoolroom, in the majority of upper- and middle-class establishments there was usually a room set aside at the top of the house as the schoolroom. Often the schoolroom would be a converted bedroom, which was sparsely furnished with redundant furniture from downstairs and an old rug on the floor. When the children were old enough to leave the nursery, they moved into the schoolroom, which was presided over by the governess. Most boys went to boarding school between seven and eight years of age, but girls were seldom educated away from home, so the governess was responsible for their education until adulthood.

Occasionally a conscientious mother would help with the lessons, or a benevolent father would drop in to check up on the boys' progress in Latin and Greek, but for the most part the parents paid little attention to what their children were being taught. In some cases the boys were educated at home until they went up to university, with a tutor coming in for special subjects that were beyond the governess's ability.

Reading, writing and arithmetic were very important, as was a foreign language and religious teachings. Strict rules applied and Victorian children were brought up with the attitude of 'spare the rod and spoil the child' and to only speak when spoken to, or to answer a direct question.

In large cities there were daily governesses, but most often the governess lived in the house in a small room at the top of the house near the children. Her position in the household was unenviable as she

The governess
was expected to
be well
educated and
cultured but she
received scant
reward.

was neither a member of the family nor a domestic servant. This caused some degree of acrimony, especially with the other staff, who could not treat her as one of themselves but knew she was never the less an employee. It could be a very lonely life as she ate upstairs with the children, was not welcome in the servants' hall and only joined the family when invited. Her background was of a certain social standing,

often a distant cousin who had never married and had no one to support her, the orphaned daughter of a clergyman or the widow of an officer.

As a governess, she had to be of high moral principles and integrity, to be

THE GOVERNESS
WAS RESPONSIBLE
FOR EDUCATING
THE GIRLS OF THE
FAMILY AND
YOUNGER BOYS.

able to instruct the children in good manners, posture and speech, and instil in them the same standard of values as held by their parents. She would act as a companion and chaperone to the girls as they grew up and encourage them in their taste and dress. She was expected to be well dressed, well educated and preferably fluent in French or another foreign language. She also needed to be able to teach the girls all the accomplishments they would need later in life, such as needlework, singing, playing the piano, drawing, painting and the art of polite conversation. Her wages, about £25.00 per annum, in no way reflected her position of responsibility and many a governess was paid nothing and expected to be grateful for being given a roof over her head.

School was not meant to be fun and neither was the governess. She never became the much-loved old retainer, like 'nanny' who was cared for by the family long after retirement, and she very often ended up a denigrated lonely spinster.

The sick-room
no talking, no g[
above all, no wh[

ould be quiet;
siping, and,
pering…

THE SICK-ROOM

ALL WOMEN ARE LIKELY, at some period of their lives, to be called on to perform the duties of a sick-nurse, and should prepare themselves as much as possible, by observation and reading, for the occasion when they may be required to perform the office. The main requirements are good-temper, compassion for suffering, sympathy with sufferers, which most women worthy of the name possess, neat-handedness, quiet manners, love of order, and cleanliness. With these qualifications there will be very little to be wished for; the desire to relieve suffering will inspire a thousand little attentions, and surmounts the disgusts which some of the offices attending the sick-room are apt to create.

Where serious illness visits a household, and protracted nursing is likely to become necessary, a professional nurse will probably be engaged who has been trained to its duties; but in some families and those not a few let us hope, the ladies of the family would oppose such an arrangement as a failure of duty on their part. There is, besides, even when a professional nurse is ultimately called in, a period of doubt and hesitation, while disease has not yet developed itself, when the patient must be attended to; and, in these cases, some of the female servants of the establishment must give their attendance in the sick-room. There are, also, slight attacks of cold,

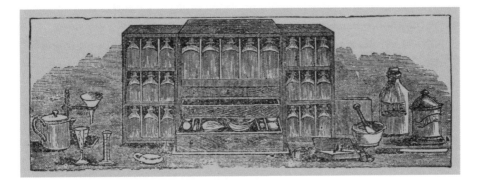

A HOME
MEDICINE CHEST
WITH REMEDIES
FOR COMMON
COMPLAINTS.

influenza, and accidents in a thousand forms, to which all are subject, where domestic nursing becomes a necessity; where disease,
though unattended with danger, is nevertheless accompanied by the
nervous irritation incident to illness, and when all the attention of
the domestic nurse becomes necessary

Although the health of many Victorian women was not robust, and
disease was rampant, there were also many ' professional invalids'.
This was often the only way women of that era could get away from
the real world and ever have time to themselves. The days could be
long and arduous and made no easier by trying to live up to the high
standards in the many manuals written on how to be the perfect
housewife and mother. For most young women, this was a new way of
life and not one they had experienced before their marriage. There
were so many rules and regulations on social behaviour, manners and
etiquette, and if you were not born to it, her new life could be very
daunting for a young bride. She not only had to be a good wife and
mother, but she also had to appear immaculately dressed and
groomed, and be the perfect hostess. She was often the educator of the
children when they were young, as well as being in command of the
house and maintaining the respect of her servants.

On top of all this she needed to have an extensive knowledge of
medicine and how to nurse the sick, as in Victorian times, hospitals
were most often only for the poor. Upper- and middle-class people
were treated and nursed at home by the mother, a relative or a servant,
if they could be spared from their other duties. If it was a serious
illness a professional nurse was employed to live in, although this was
not an acceptable alternative to many women as ' professed' nurses
were disliked and distrusted, and most women felt duty bound to do
the nursing themselves. To call the doctor to the house was very
expensive and his word was law, never to be questioned. He was also
regarded with suspicion in many instances, as his treatment was often
radical, more painful than the illness and very often to no avail.

VICTORIAN
WOMEN WERE
EXPECTED TO HAVE
SOME KNOWLEDGE
OF MEDICINE AND
NURSING IN
ADDITION TO ALL
THEIR OTHER
SKILLS.

Professional nurses need not only the qualifications already named
in addition to their training; they should be physically strong, have
good health, nerves well under control, and be sure that nursing to
them is a congenial occupation. What a
friend or relative can do for one she holds
dear in the time of sickness, the taxing of
strength, the loss of sleep that she makes
light of in such a case, is no proof that
she is fitted for the post of a professional
nurse. The very self-sacrifice is against
this, for a nurse must do what she does in
a business-like way, she must not over-
fatigue herself, should eat, drink and sleep well, and take regular
exercise; while it should not be (as it is so often to the amateur)
actual suffering to see pain inflicted when it is necessary that any
operation be performed. She should be, like the surgeon, able to
think of the future good instead of the present suffering.

To some nervous, highly organised persons this would be impossible, and they are therefore unsuited for nursing as a business,
although they may be the most devoted and patient attendants upon
those they love.

Nurse's dress

A nurse's dress should be of some washing material that neither
rustles nor crackles; her shoes should be soft ones that do not creak,
her sleeves should be loose enough to roll back, and she should have
a plentiful supply of large white aprons. A professional nurse
should wear a neat white cap. Suffering people are apt to be
impressed by trifles, such as a black dress having a gloomy look,

while a bright one has a cheering effect, and we ourselves prefer to see a pretty cotton gown, for example, in a sick room, than a sombre, black looking one, for, beside the fact of the former being pleasanter to the eye, it has the additional advantage of not carrying infection as the woollen gown might.

FOLLOWING ORDERS

Doctors' orders are never disregarded by a nurse worthy of the name. Should she be watching the case and think any other treatment or diet would be beneficial to the patient, she should not act upon her own opinion, but state it to the doctor. She should always report to him any change she observes in the patient, which she should be watchful to detect. The hearty co-operation of a nurse is of incalculable help to a doctor.

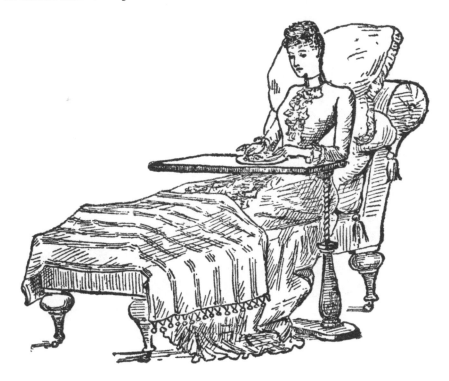

AN INVALID TABLE ON A STAND COULD BE SWUNG OVER A COUCH OR BED, PROVIDING A TRAY FOR PLACING MEALS AND DRINKS.

[*267*]

A GENTLE,
UNDERSTANDING
MANNER WAS
ESSENTIAL IN THE
SICK-ROOM.

"Patients," says Miss Nightingale, "are sometimes starved in the midst of plenty, from want of attention to the ways which alone make it possible for them to take food. A spoonful of beef-tea, or arrowroot and wine, or some other light nourishing diet, should be given every hour, for the patient's stomach will reject large supplies. In weak patients there is often a nervous difficulty in swallowing, which is much increased if food is not ready and presented at the moment when it is wanted; the nurse should be able to discriminate, and know when this moment is approaching." Never bring a large plateful to an invalid; let it be, if anything, rather less than more than you think he will take, a little can easily be added; but the sight of much food will sometimes prevent a patient taking any.

Beef-tea is useful and relishing but possesses little nourishment; when evaporated, it presents a teaspoon of solid meat to a pint of water. Eggs are not the equivalent to the same weight of meat. Arrowroot is less nourishing than flour. Butter is the lightest and most digestive kind of fat. Cream, in some diseases cannot be replaced.

A CURE FOR STAMMERING

WHERE there is no malformation of the organs of articulation, stammering may be remedied by reading aloud with the teeth closed. This should be practised for two hours a day, for three or four months. The advocate of this simple remedy says, 'I can speak with certainty of its utility.'

Many romantic novels and films of today depict the delicate female invalid reclining gracefully on a chaise-longue, surrounded by flowers, books and pretty knick-knacks, but in fact the sick-room in a Victorian house was more often a sparse, austere room with the carpets removed and only the bare necessities of furniture remaining.

THE SICK-ROOM

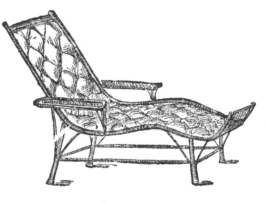

In the first stage of sickness, while doubt and a little perplexity hang over the household as to the nature of the sickness, there are some things about which no doubt exist: the patient's room must be kept in a perfectly pure state, and arrangements made for proper attendance; for the first canon of nursing, according to Florence Nightingale, its apostle, is to "keep the air the patient breathes as pure as the external air, without chilling him." This can be done without any preparation which might alarm the patient; with proper windows, open fireplaces, and a supply of fuel, the room may be as fresh as it is outside, and kept at a temperature suitable for the patient's state.

Windows, however, must be opened from above, and not from below, and draughts avoided; cool air admitted beneath the patient's head chills the lower strata and the floor. The careful nurse will keep the door shut when the window is open; she will also take care that the patient is not placed between the door and the open window, nor between the open fire-place and the window. If confined to bed, she will see that the bed is placed in a thoroughly ventilated part of the room, but out of the current of air which is produced by the momentary

TWO KINDS OF INVALID CHAIRS FOR USE WHEN THE PATIENT WAS WELL ENOUGH TO LEAVE HIS BED.

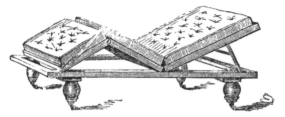

opening of doors, as well as out of the line of draught between the window and the open chimney, and that the temperature of the room is kept about 64°. Where it is necessary to admit air by the door, the windows should be closed; but there are few circumstances in which good air can be obtained through the chamber door; through it, on the contrary, the gases generated in the lower parts of the house are likely to be drawn into the invalid chamber. These precautions taken, and plain nourishing diet, such as the patient desires, furnished, probably little more can be done, unless more serious symptoms present themselves; in which case medical advice will be sought.

Under no circumstances is ventilation of the sick-room

> ### INTOXICATION
>
> *Treatment.*
> ——
>
> WHEN LOSS of consciousness has occurred from this cause, give an emetic of mustard and water (a tablespoon in tepid water) or twenty grains of sulphate of zinc or powdered ipecacuanha. Remove to a warm atmosphere and give strong tea or coffee.

so essential as in cases of febrile diseases, usually considered infectious; such as typhus and puerperal fevers, influenza, hooping-cough, small- and chicken-pox, scarlet fever, measles, and erysipelas: all these are considered communicable through the air; but there is little danger of infection being thus communicated, provided the room is kept thoroughly ventilated. On the contrary, if this essential be neglected, the power of infection is greatly increased and concentrated in the confined and impure air; it settles upon the clothes of the attendants and visitors, especially where they are of wool, and is frequently communicated to other families in this manner. The comfort of feverish patients, and indeed of most sick persons, is greatly increased by being sponged with tepid water, in which camphorated spirit is dropped. A teaspoon should be poured into a

TO CURE A COLD

*(A most Efficacious and Simple
Remedy for a Severe Cold
in the Head.)*

—

TAKE A SMALL BASIN, put into it boiling water and strong camphorated spirit, in the proportion of 1 teaspoon of spirit to half a pint of water. Wring out a sponge in this as hot as possible, and apply it to the nose or mouth; draw in the steam with the nose first and then the mouth; swallow the steam, and, to prevent any escape, cover the head with a flannel. Repeat this operation for some time, having another hot sponge when the first gets cool. Sponges so wrung out in the same mixture may with great benefit be applied outwards to the throat and chest.

Camphorated sal-volatile is a good medicine for a cold, 30 drops in a wineglass of warm water several times in the course of a day.

quart of water, and a patient may be sponged every hour or two, in warm weather.

Under all circumstances, therefore, the sick-room should be kept as fresh and sweet as the open air, while the temperature is kept up by artificial heat, taking care that the fire burns clear, and gives out no smoke into the room; that the room is perfectly clean, wiped over with a damp cloth every day, if boarded; and swept, after sprinkling with damp tea-leaves, or other aromatic leaves, if carpeted; that all utensils are emptied and cleaned as soon as used, and not once in four-and-twenty hours, as is sometimes done.

"A slop-pail," Miss Nightingale says, "should never enter a sick-room; everything should be carried direct to the water-closet, emptied there, and brought up clean; in the best hospitals the slop-pail is unknown." "I do not approve," says Miss Nightingale, "of making housemaids of nurses,— that would be a waste of means; but I have seen surgical sisters, women whose hands were worth to them two or three guineas a week, down on their hands and knees, scouring a room or hut, because they thought it was not fit for their patients: these women had the true nurse-spirit."

Bad smells are sometimes met by sprinkling a little liquid chloride of lime on the floor; fumigation by burning pastilles is also a common expedient for the purification of the sick-room. They are useful, but only in the sense hinted at by the medical lecturer, who commenced his lecture thus:– "Fumigations, gentlemen, are of essential importance; they make so abominable a smell, that they compel you to open the windows and admit fresh air." In this sense they are useful, but ineffectual unless the cause be removed, and fresh air admitted.

The sick-room should be quiet; no talking, no gossiping, and, above all, no whispering,—this is absolute cruelty to the patient; he thinks his complaint the subject, and strains his ear painfully to catch the sound. No rustling of dresses, nor creaking shoes either; where the carpets are taken up, the nurse should wear list shoes, or some other noiseless material, and her dress should be of soft material that does not rustle. Miss Nightingale denounces crinoline, and quotes Lord Melbourne on the subject of women in the

TO CURE A COLD

PUT A LARGE teacupful of linseed, with ¼lb. of sun raisins and 2oz. of stick liquorice, into 2 quarts of soft water, and let it simmer over a slow fire till reduced to one quart; add to it ¼lb. of pounded sugar-candy, a tablespoon of old rum, and a tablespoon of the best white-wine vinegar, or lemon juice. The rum and vinegar should be added as the decoction is taken; for, if they are put in first, the whole soon becomes flat and less efficacious. The dose is half a pint, made warm, on going to bed; and a little may be taken whenever the cough is troublesome. The worst cold is generally cured by this remedy in two or three days; and, if taken in time, is considered infallible.

A cold on the chest

—

A FLANNEL dipped in boiling water, and sprinkled with turpentine, laid on the chest as quickly as possible, will relieve the most severe cold or hoarseness.

[*273*]

HYSTERIA

THIS MAY manifest itself by intense sobbing or immoderate laughter, or these may alternate with one another. There is frequently wild tossing about of the arms, the hair is dishevelled, the face is generally pale and complaint is made of a suffocating feeling in the throat.

Treatment
—

The patient must be spoken to kindly, yet firmly, and be told to stop any eccentricities. Loosen the dress and remove anything tight from the neck. Give a teaspoon of spirit of sal-volatile in water. If no heed is taken to what is said, dash cold water upon the face.

sick-room, who said, "I would rather have men about me, when ill, than women; it requires very strong health to put up with women." Ungrateful man! But absolute quiet is necessary in the sick-room. Never let the patient be waked out of his first sleep by noise, never roused by anything like a surprise. Always sit in the apartment, so that the patient has you in view, and that it is not necessary for him to turn in speaking to you. Never keep a patient standing; never speak to one while moving. Never lean on the sick-bed. Above all, be calm and decisive with the patient, and prevent all noises over-head. A careful nurse, when a patient leaves his bed, will open the sheets wide, and throw the clothes back so as to thoroughly air the bed. She will avoid drying or airing anything damp in the sick-room.

"It is another fallacy," says Florence Nightingale, "to suppose that night air is injurious; a great authority told me that, in London, the air is never so good as after ten o'clock, when smoke has diminished; but then it must be air from without, not within, and not air vitiated by gaseous airs."

"A great fallacy prevails also," she says, in another section, "about flowers poisoning the air of the sick-room; no one ever saw them over-crowding the sick-room; but if they did, they actually

SOME SIMPLE
METHODS
OF BANDAGING
INJURIES, AS
RECOMMENDED BY
MRS BEETON.

[*274*]

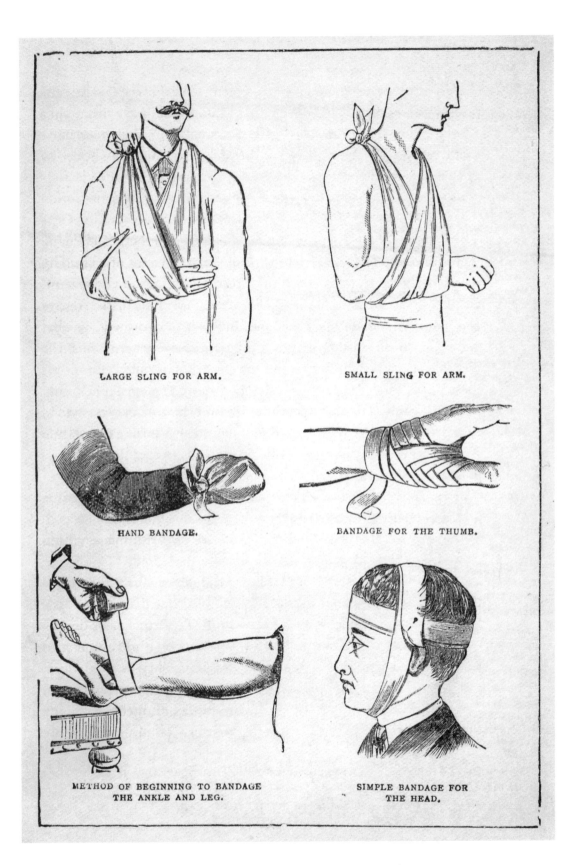

LARGE SLING FOR ARM.

SMALL SLING FOR ARM.

HAND BANDAGE.

BANDAGE FOR THE THUMB.

METHOD OF BEGINNING TO BANDAGE
THE ANKLE AND LEG.

SIMPLE BANDAGE FOR
THE HEAD.

absorb carbonic acid, and give off oxygen." Cut flowers also decompose water, and produce oxygen gas. Lilies, and some other very odorous plants, may perhaps give out smells unsuited to a close room, while the atmosphere of the sick-room should always be fresh and natural.

CHANGING SHEETS

There are several ways of changing sheets, but perhaps there is no more simple and easy one than we here illustrate, that of rolling up the dirty sheet in a narrow roll till it reaches the side of the patient, treating the clean sheet in the same way, that is rolling it from end to end half way across. The clean and dirty roll are now side by side, and a very little shifting will take the patient over them, when the dirty sheet can be withdrawn and the clean one unrolled and spread in its place. Under sheets for a sick bed should be small ones, only just large enough to tuck in at the sides, and should never be wound round the bolster. A very hard pillow should be used as a foundation when it is necessary to make a pile for the patient to sit up in bed, as in cases of bronchitis.

TO APPLY LEECHES

SHOULD they not bite at once put the spot of blood obtained by a slight prick of the finger on the place. When filled they usually roll off; but if it is necessary to detach them they must not be pulled, but a little salt must be shaken over them, which will make them release their hold. Should too much bleeding follow apply a little powdered alum.

For a helpless patient a draw-sheet is often needed, which may be made with a large sheet folded lengthwise to about a yard wide. This should be laid across the middle of the bed over a mackintosh, with one end reaching only to the side of the bed, and the surplus at the other formed into a roll that can be unwound as the sheet is drawn from the other side. Be most careful to have this draw-sheet so firmly fixed with safety-pins or by being tucked under the mattress that it will not ruck or crease, and so avoid great discomfort, if not pain, to the patient.

Fresh smooth sheets and cool pillows afford great comfort to most invalids, and a good nurse will be on the watch for opportunities of replacing a pillow and changing or smoothing a sheet when these offices can be performed without inconveniencing or disturbing her patient.

CAUTIONS IN VISITING SICK-ROOMS

NEVER VENTURE into a sick-room if you are in a violent perspiration (if circumstances require your continuance there), for the moment your body becomes cold, it is in a state likely to absorb the infection, and give you the disease. Nor visit a sick person (especially if the complaint be of a contagious nature) with an empty stomach; as this disposes the system more readily to receive the contagion. In attending a sick person, place yourself where the air passes from the door or window to the bed of the diseased, not betwixt the diseased person and any fire that is in the room, as the heat of the fire will draw the infectious vapour in that direction, and you would run much danger from breathing it.

CONVALESCENCE

In this stage the patient is often more difficult to manage than when seriously ill, he is more wayward and fanciful, more easily put out, and more easily impressed by his surroundings. The room should be made as bright and pretty as possible; he should be tempted to eat what is best for him, and firmly refused what would be detrimental. Anything that can be done to while away the long hours of weakness should be tried, whether it be reading aloud, or by the nurse engaging herself with some occupation that it would be pleasant for the invalid to watch.

[277]

She who makes her
children happy, who
from vice and trains
virtue, is a much gr
than ladies describe

ısband and her
eclaims the one
ıp the other to
ter character
ı novels.

INDEX

↠ L ↞

↠ M ↞

AUTHOR'S
ACKNOWLEDGEMENTS

MY THANKS to Susan Haynes, friend of many years and editorial director, who had more faith in my ability than I did. The dedicated team at Weidenfeld & Nicolson, including design director, David Rowley, picture researcher Bronagh Woods, talented designer Ken Wilson, and very special editor, Jinny Johnson, who somehow managed to put all my ideas and words together to create the finished article.

My thanks also to Will Goddard who, on several occasions during this project, saved my sanity and my computer from both going out the window. To my son Duncan Fairfax and friends, Judy Anderson and Ian Dixon for their help and encouragement, and to Erica Macpherson for her early copy of Mrs Beeton.

Most of all, my thanks to my husband, Michael Burton, without whom there would be no book. His love, support, his daily editing, helpful input and his reassurance that I would not be beaten by Beeton.

PICTURE CREDITS

EVERY EFFORT has been made to trace and contact all copyright holders. The publishers would be pleased to rectify any errors or omissions brought to their attention at the earliest opportunity.

GETTY IMAGES: 2, 42, 110;

MARY EVANS PICTURE LIBRARY: 4, 8, 9, 11, 21, 23, 24, 31, 32, 36, 57, 69, 71, 84, 127, 137, 148, 173, 176 (top), 178, 179. 182, 186, 213, 225, 230, 239, 248;

BRIDGEMAN IMAGES: 6, 105;

The Apartments of the House, Joseph Crouch and Edmund Butler (Birmingham: 1900): 15, 20, 74;

The Book of Household Management, Mrs. Isabella Beeton (London: Ward, Lock & Co., Limited, 1899): 16, 29, 33, 34 (top and bottom), 35, 41, 44, 45, 46, 48, 49, 50, 52, 53, 62, 63, 83, 85, 87, 90, 97, 98, 99, 100, 101, 102, 103, 104, 106, 109, 111, 113, 117, 123, 128, 129, 130, 131, 132, 133, 135, 139, 141, 145, 146, 147, 149, 150, 151, 152, 153, 154, 155, 156, 157, 158, 159, 160, 161, 162, 163, 164, 165, 166, 172, 174, 175, 176 (bottom), 181, 183, 184, 185, 187, 191, 198, 199, 200, 204, 206, 207, 212, 214, 219, 226, 227, 231, 238, 240, 242, 243, 249, 250, 252, 255, 256, 263, 270, 275;

Vanity Fair, W.M Thackeray (London, Dent, 1908): 17;

From Kitchen to Garret: Hints for Young Householders, J.E. Panton (London, 1888): 18, 19, 108, 115, 215;

The Home Book of Pleasure and Instruction, Mrs. R. Valentine (ed.), (London: Frederick Warne, 1867): 58, 253, 258, 259, 265:

Punch Ltd., *www.punch.co.uk*: 81; 118

West Sussex County Council Archives: 82, 93;

The Servants Magazine (October, 1869): 86;

Christmas Books, W.M. Thackeray (London: Caxton, 1906): 88;

V&A IMAGES: 91, 237;

THE ILLUSTRATED LONDON NEWS PICTURE LIBRARY: 114;

The Parent's Assistant or Stories for Children, Maria Edgeworth (London: Macmillan, 1897): 125, 241:

Family Magazine (London: Cassell, 1887) / Heritage Image Partnership: 180;

The Country House Servant, Pamela Sambrook (Gloucester: Sutton Publishing, 1999): 188, 197;

The Laundrymaid, Her Duties and How to Perform Them (Houlston's Industrial Library, 1877): 201;

The Art and Practice of Laundry Work, Margaret Rankin, (London: Blackie and Co, 1911): 203;

Good Words (London: 1868) / Heritage Image Partnership: 222;

Domestic Pests, L. Hunter (London, John Bale, 1938): 226;

The Book of Snobs, W.M. Thackeray (London, Macmillan, 1911): 229;

Illustration by Phiz from *Bleak House*, Charles Dickens, from *The Dickens Picture Book: A Record of Dickens Illustrations*, J.A. Hammerton (London: Educational Book Company, 1910); 268.

First published in Great Britain in 2007
by Weidenfeld & Nicolson

10 9 8 7 6 5 4 3 2 1

A CIP catalogue record for this book is available from the British Library.

ISBN: 978 0 297 84460 0

*The Orion Publishing Group's policy is to use
papers that are natural, renewable and recyclable products
and made from wood grown in sustainable forests.
The logging and manufacturing processes are expected
to conform to the environmental regulations
of the country of origin.*

Design director DAVID ROWLEY
Editorial director SUSAN HAYNES
Designed by KEN WILSON | POINT918
Edited by JINNY JOHNSON
Picture research by BRONAGH WOODS
Index by ELIZABETH WIGGANS

Printed in Great Britain

WEIDENFELD & NICOLSON
The Orion Publishing Group Ltd
Orion House
5 Upper St Martin's Lane
London WC2H 9EA
www.orionbooks.co.uk
An Hachette Livre UK Company